LIFE

The Year

LIFE

The Year in Pictures
1998

EDITOR Killian Jordan

PICTURE EDITOR Azurea Lee Dudley

ART DIRECTOR David Israel, 2x4

DESIGN CONSULTANT Neal T. Boulton

ASSOCIATE PICTURE EDITOR Donna Aceto

ASSISTANT PICTURE EDITOR Dot McMahon

PHOTO RESEARCH Lauren Steel

WRITER Marlene McCampbell

WRITER-REPORTER Susan Feinberg

REPORTER Hildegard Anderson

COPY EDITOR Kathleen Berger

PAGE CODER Al Rufino

And all members of
the **LIFE** Copy Department

Time Inc. Home Entertainment

PRESIDENT David Gitow

DIRECTOR, CONTINUITIES AND SINGLE SALES David Arfine

DIRECTOR, CONTINUITIES AND RETENTION Michael Barrett

DIRECTOR, NEW PRODUCTS Alicia Longobardo

GROUP PRODUCT MANAGERS
Robert Fox, Jennifer McLyman

PRODUCT MANAGERS Christopher Berzolla,
Roberta Harris, Stacy Hirschberg,
Kenneth Maehlum, Daniel Melore

MANAGER, RETAIL AND NEW MARKETS Thomas Mifsud

ASSOCIATE PRODUCT MANAGERS Carlos Jimenez,
Daria Raehse, Betty Su, Niki Viswanathan,
Lauren Zaslansky, Cheryl Zukowski

ASSISTANT PRODUCT MANAGERS
Jennifer Dowell, Meredith Shelley

EDITORIAL OPERATIONS DIRECTOR John Calvano

BOOK PRODUCTION MANAGER Jessica McGrath

ASSISTANT BOOK PRODUCTION MANAGER Joseph Napolitano

FULFILLMENT DIRECTOR Michelle Gudema

ASSISTANT FULFILLMENT MANAGER Richard Perez

FINANCIAL DIRECTOR Tricia Griffin

FINANCIAL MANAGER Amy Maselli

ASSISTANT FINANCIAL MANAGER Steven Sandonato

MARKETING ASSISTANT Ann Gillespie

SPECIAL THANKS TO Anna Yelenskaya

COPYRIGHT 1999
TIME INC. HOME ENTERTAINMENT

PUBLISHED BY

Books

TIME INC.
1271 AVENUE OF THE AMERICAS
NEW YORK, NEW YORK 10020

FIRST EDITION

HARD COVER ISBN: 1-883013-60-7
ISSN: 1092-0463

"LIFE" IS A TRADEMARK OF TIME INC.

We welcome your comments
and suggestions about **LIFE** Books.
Please write to us at:

LIFE Books
Attention: Book Editors
PO Box 11016
Des Moines, IA 50336-1016

If you would like to order any of
our Hard Cover Collector's Edition books,
please call us at 1-800-327-6388.
(Monday through Friday, 7:00 a.m.–
8:00 p.m. or Saturday, 7:00 a.m.–
6:00 p.m., Central Time.)

PRINTED IN THE UNITED STATES OF AMERICA

COVER PHOTOGRAPHS
FRONT
SOSA & McGWIRE: SUE OGROCKI/SIPA PRESS
THE CLINTONS: GARY HERSHORN/REUTERS-ARCHIVE PHOTOS
FRANK SINATRA: SID AVERY/MPTV
HURRICANE GEORGES: DAVE MARTIN/AP
POPE JOHN PAUL II & FIDEL CASTRO: GIANNI GIANSANTI/SYGMA
IRISH FUNERAL: DYLAN MARTINEZ/REUTERS
BACK
PRESIDENT CLINTON: ROBERT TRIPPETT/SIPA PRESS

In
Pictures
1998

CONTENTS

President Clinton, from videotaped grand jury testimony, broadcast to the public on September 21

WINTER

Deep Freeze
The fiercest ice storms in decades lashed the northeastern U.S. and eastern Canada in early January. Ice-encrusted power lines buckled; utility poles, like these in upstate New York, snapped like toothpicks; millions of residents were stranded without electricity. It was a dramatic beginning to a year of extreme weather.

SPEED LIMIT 35

JAN. 6 The unmanned Lunar Prospector blasts off from Cape Canaveral on a yearlong, $63 million mission to **explore the moon's surface** for frozen water, minerals and gases that might help sustain a human colony.

JAN. 8 World Trade Center bomber Ramzi Ahmed Yousef is sentenced to 240 years in prison. "**I am a terrorist,** and I am proud of it," Yousef tells a New York court.

JAN. 13 Iraqi President Saddam Hussein blocks a United Nations **weapons inspection team,** led by American Scott Ritter, from investigating "sensitive" government-controlled sites for evidence of illegal biological, chemical or nuclear weapons technology.

JAN. 13 About to lose its lucrative *Seinfeld* to retirement and the Super Bowl to other networks, NBC agrees to pay nearly $13 million an episode— **the most ever spent** for a television series—for its hit drama *E.R.* Later the same day, ABC and ESPN negotiate to keep *Monday Night Football* for $1.15 billion a season, another record-breaking deal.

Mass Appeal
A spiffed-up Fidel Castro, and many jubilant, flag-waving Cubans, made time to greet Pope John Paul II on his arrival in Havana. It was the first papal visit to the island, the Western Hemisphere's last communist country. Both aging leaders brought missionary zeal to their speeches: the pontiff pleading for human rights, Castro bitterly denouncing the 36-year U.S. trade embargo.

9

JAN. 16 NASA announces that John Glenn, who in 1962 was **the first American to orbit Earth,** has become its "newest and oldest astronaut." The 76-year-old senator will board the space shuttle *Discovery* in October as a payload specialist.

JAN. 16 Three federal judges secretly grant Whitewater independent counsel Kenneth Starr authority to probe whether President Clinton and Vernon Jordan urged a former **White House intern** named Monica Lewinsky to lie, in a signed affidavit, about her relationship with Clinton. Lewinsky's January 7 affidavit was part of a sexual harassment suit against Clinton by former Arkansas state employee Paula Jones.

JAN. 16 Philip Morris Companies and other cigarette manufacturers agree to pay the state of Texas about $15 billion over 25 years in the **largest-ever tobacco settlement.** Texas had sued to recover Medicaid money spent on smoking-related illnesses. Since 1994, 40 states and Puerto Rico have filed lawsuits against the tobacco industry.

Palm Before the Storm

As accusations of an affair (and cover-up) with a 21-year-old White House intern swirled about him, President Bill Clinton glad-handed congressional pages after his January 27 State of the Union address. Gripped by the scandal, a huge TV audience had tuned in, but the embattled Commander in Chief stuck to affairs of state only. His delivery delivered: Clinton's job-approval rating promptly soared to its highest ever.

JAN. 17 Paula Jones's lawyers question President Clinton for nearly six hours regarding allegations of sexual misconduct. During the session, Clinton **denies under oath** having "sexual relations" with Monica Lewinsky.

JAN. 21 Internet rumors propel Clinton's alleged affair with Lewinsky into a full-blown scandal. Major news organizations report on Starr's expanded investigation and audiotapes his office received from former White House aide Linda Tripp. Tripp **secretly recorded conversations** with Lewinsky that include intimate details of Lewinsky's relationship with the President. Clinton tells PBS, "I did not ask anyone to tell anything other than the truth. There is no improper relationship."

JAN. 25 The Denver Broncos upset the Green Bay Packers 31–24 in **Super Bowl XXXII.** It is a dream come true for the Broncos' brilliant quarterback John Elway, 37, who had been haunted by three Super Bowl losses.

Going Home

In the media frenzy following the initial allegations of a presidential affair, people tended to see Monica Lewinsky as either a vamp or a victim. But fleeing Washington in early February to visit her father, a Los Angeles physician, she was someone else— a tearful daughter craving a respite from notoriety. Alas, nearly 50 reporters shared the moment as Bernard Lewinsky and his second wife embraced his child.

13

JAN. 27 Appearing on NBC's *Today,* First Lady Hillary Rodham Clinton calls the Lewinsky scandal the product of a "vast right-wing conspiracy." The previous night, wagging his finger at television cameras, President Clinton had delivered his most memorable denial to date: "I did not have sexual relations with **that woman,** Miss Lewinsky. I never told anybody to lie, not a single time. Never."

JAN. 29 A homemade bomb kills an off-duty police officer outside the entrance to an abortion clinic in Birmingham, Ala., and seriously injures a nurse. Within weeks, Eric Robert Rudolph, 31, becomes the FBI's sole suspect and **the target of a colossal manhunt** in North Carolina.

FEB. 2 Introducing the first balanced budget in 30 years, President Clinton says, "This budget marks the end of an era, **an end to decades of deficits** that have shackled our economy." Republicans criticize the plan, particularly Clinton's proposal to expand government programs, largely with revenues from a proposed settlement of health claims against the tobacco industry.

Swell Job

Surf's up! *Way* **up. Powered by El Niño storms, building-size avalanches of water walloped competitors in Baja California's Reef Brazil championship. Taylor Knox, 26, paddled to the crest of one monster wave, balanced and sped down the glassy slope to victory. His prize for catching the 52-footer, the biggest of the season? A totally tubular $50,000.**

FEB. 4 An earthquake in northern Afghanistan, followed by devastating landslides, interrupts a civil war and ultimately leaves about **4,500 people dead and 30,000 homeless.** Deep snow and fog in the remote province disrupt major relief efforts for nearly two weeks.

FEB. 7 Japanese figure skater Midori Ito lights the Olympic flame in front of 2,450 athletes from 72 countries and 50,000 spectators to open the **XVIII Winter Games** in Nagano, Japan. The Games will earn CBS disappointing ratings, which critics will attribute to poor coverage, a 14-hour time difference, weather delays and a shortage of dominant American athletes.

FEB. 10 After intense campaigning by the Christian Coalition, Maine voters repeal a 1997 **gay rights law** by a slim margin, making their state the first to abandon such legislation.

Lost Cause

"I love all of you very much," said born-again Christian and convicted killer Karla Faye Tucker, 38, moments before her execution by lethal injection in Huntsville, Tex. Under the influence of drugs and alcohol, Tucker, then 23, and her boyfriend Daniel Ryan Garrett brutally murdered two people with a pickax. (Garrett died of liver disease before his death sentence could be carried out.) Though her death row repentance drew an extraordinary mix of supporters— the ACLU, televangelist Pat Robertson, one of the victim's brothers, the prison chaplain Tucker married two years ago— her last-chance clemency appeal failed. Tucker is only the second woman put to death in the U.S. since the reinstatement of capital punishment in 1976.

17

FEB. 23 A devastating storm rips through California in a bizarre 24 hours of torrential **rain, tornadoes, mudslides, flash floods and heavy snow.** It is one of the deadliest El Niño attacks on the state this winter.

FEB. 25 Bob Dylan, John Fogerty and Elton John are among the **old-time rock 'n' rollers** who win Grammys at the 40th annual awards ceremony. One of the evening's most stirring performances is from Aretha Franklin. A last-minute substitute for Luciano Pavarotti, she sings Puccini's aria "Nessun dorma."

FEB. 26 Talk-show host Oprah Winfrey wins a lawsuit filed against her by four Texas ranchers who claimed her 1996 program on **mad cow disease** cost them $11 million and sent the cattle industry into a tailspin. During her show, Winfrey had vowed never to eat another hamburger.

Early Mourning

Thirty thousand mourners in Kosovo wept for Qerim Muriqi, 52, shot when Serbian police opened fire on ethnic Albanians peacefully demonstrating against recent massacres that had left more than 80 dead. The Serbs claimed their deadly sweeps were necessary to "liquidate" the Kosovo Liberation Army, separatists fighting for an independent state for the Albanians, who make up 90 percent of the province's population.

18

FEB. 28 Angered by an ambush that killed two comrades, Serbian police launch a bloody campaign to wipe out "terrorist gangs" in the Yugoslav province of Kosovo. In the aftermath, the U.S. accuses Serbia of **"ethnic cleansing"** in Kosovo.

MAR. 2 The U.N. Security Council unanimously approves a deal with Iraq, brokered by Secretary-General Kofi Annan, that will open up restricted "presidential" sites to **weapons inspectors.** The council's resolution threatens "severest consequences" if President Saddam Hussein defies the accord but does not grant military carte blanche to the U.S.

MAR. 2 New images from the American spacecraft Galileo reveal that Jupiter's moon Europa may contain **the right conditions for life.** The pictures show evidence of a liquid ocean and interior heat.

Dead Fall

Under crystalline skies in the Italian Alps, a U.S. Marine fighter jet severed the cable of a big yellow ski gondola, plunging 19 European vacationers and the ski lift operator 300 feet to their deaths on this snowy valley floor. Italy's prime minister termed the incident "an act of tragic recklessness"—the jet was flying below the minimum authorized altitude. Both pilot and navigator face a court-martial early next year on charges of involuntary manslaughter.

21

MAR. 4 Just three months after Golden State Warrior Latrell Sprewell, 27, was fired by his team and suspended for a year by the NBA for **choking and punching his coach,** an arbitrator reinstates Sprewell's contract and reduces his suspension to 68 games. "We're more than a little disappointed," says NBA Commissioner David Stern. So was Sprewell: He will later sue the Warriors and the NBA for $30 million in damages and lost wages.

MAR. 5 The appointment of Air Force Lt. Col. Eileen Collins, **the first woman to command a space shuttle** mission, is announced by Hillary Rodham Clinton. Collins will lead the *Columbia* crew on its December mission to launch a large X-ray telescope.

MAR. 12 One day after scientists at an international astronomical agency predicted that on October 26, 2028, a mile-wide asteroid could hit Earth and cause massive global destruction, new calculations reveal **the likelihood of collision** to be "effectively zero."

Fancy Footwork

Imelda Marcos, 68, onetime first lady of the Philippines, tossed her shoe into the ring for the presidency but withdrew soon after this high-stepping display in March, part of International Women's Day festivities. In October, following a 13-year government investigation into the alleged billions in hidden assets of deposed dictator Ferdinand Marcos, his spry widow agreed to settle claims involving "only" $540 million.

22

MAR. 13 A military jury finds Sgt. Maj. Gene McKinney, **the Army's top enlisted soldier,** guilty of obstructing justice but acquits him of 18 sexual misconduct charges. McKinney's sentence—a reprimand and reduction in rank—is a disappointment to his six female accusers.

MAR. 15 On *60 Minutes,* Kathleen Willey describes unwanted sexual advances made to her by President Clinton during a meeting in his White House study. Although **Willey's account contradicts Clinton's sworn version**, polls show the President's approval ratings near historic highs the next day.

MAR. 23 In a surprise announcement, the German media giant Bertelsmann AG— which already owns Bantam Doubleday Dell—agrees to purchase American publisher **Random House** for an estimated $1.4 billion, creating the largest English-language book-publishing company in the world.

Ambush in Arkansas

"I have a lot of killing to do," said Mitchell Johnson, 13, who may have been angry about a girl's rejection. It is alleged that his 11-year-old schoolmate Andrew Golden set off a Jonesboro middle school fire alarm to lure students outside, and that the pair fatally gunned down four girls and an English teacher. Anguished paramedics at the scene illustrate how shattering it is when children murder children.

25

MAR. 29 Going into college basketball's March Madness with the best record (39–0) in NCAA history, Tennessee wins the women's championship by trouncing Louisiana Tech 93–75. "That is the **greatest women's basketball team** I've ever seen," says defeated Tech coach Leon Barmore.

MAR. 30 March Madness, Part 2: Kentucky makes **a startling comeback** against Utah to claim the men's NCAA title with a 78–69 victory.

MAR. 31 The University of California at Berkeley announces **a sharp decline** in black and Hispanic students among its incoming freshman class, the first chosen without preference to race, ethnicity or gender in two decades. The low numbers are a result of a new state constitutional amendment, Proposition 209, that outlaws affirmative action in public institutions.

Soggy Spring

Thanks to El Niño, the spring of 1998 was one of the wettest on record in parts of the country. Swollen by four days of torrential rains, normally unassuming Beaver Dam Creek tore through a levee in March and inundated Elba (pop. 4,000), Ala. It happened so fast that authorities had no time to warn the townsfolk, and many had to be evacuated by Army helicopters. Over the weekend, storms across the region—including a tempest that dropped seven-inch hailstones on Shreveport, La.—killed at least nine people. Said an emergency-management official: "I think we've emptied the Gulf of Mexico over these southern states the past few days."

HOT WHEELS

Power mirrors? Side-impact air bags? In a Bug? What's going on here? It's new-tech nostalgia and, in this case, it begins at $15,900. Twenty years after production was halted, the Beetle is back—a little bit sleeker but still, as its maker claims, pretty huggable.

THE WINTER REPORT

JANUARY FEBRUARY MARCH

As we rang in the new year, we tried to focus on what was most important: renewing our spirits and looking forward to 1998 with energy and resolve. We were shocked by the death of the incorrigibly ebullient Sonny Bono (page 138), taken aback by the lashing fury of ice storms across the northeastern part of the country (page 6) but buoyed a bit by the apparently unsinkable *Titanic* (page 32). World events loomed large as well. There was just one odd distraction: a rumor that the President had had an affair with a White House intern. What a relief when he simply, categorically, denied it.

NUMERO UNO

John Berendt's *Midnight in the Garden of Good and Evil* set a new nonfiction-best-seller-list record: 216 weeks. One character, savvy transvestite The Lady Chablis, is seen here in her normal state—cross-dressed to the nines.

"You could actually hear the ground creeping."

Firefighter Scott Brown, of Orange County, Calif., after a hillside, weakened by El Niño rains, collapsed and demolished two houses and nine condominiums

TACO BELLE

He's the hottest eight pounds in show business this year, and he's a she named Gidget. Her appearances in Taco Bell ads have earned her a large (well, anything's large when you're 11 inches tall) following and just a touch of diva-ness: She is accompanied on all photographic shoots by her faithful retainer, a stuffed animal named Mrs. Hedgehog.

"If you can't be rude or annoying in a mental hospital, where can you be rude or annoying?"

Actor Kirk Douglas's son Eric, when he was cleared of charges of harassing a young girl at a psychiatric hospital

FULL-TILT BOOGIE

It is customary for the hosts of the Winter Olympics to treat the world to opening ceremonies that illuminate local culture and history. The bulky grace of these sumo wrestlers, however, was an unexpected pleasure. And perhaps a sign of things to come: Nagano, Japan, turned out to be a most welcoming and gracious venue, a fact not readily apparent from the trouble-plagued TV coverage of events.

"This is the kindest cut of all."

Wayne Pacelle, of the Humane Society of the U.S., on plans to have Buddy, the First Dog, neutered

GOOD CLEAN FUN?

One January week of *Jerry Springer Show* topics:

I'm Having A Secret Affair!

Stop Sleeping With My Lover!

Jerry Rescues A 1,200-Pound Couple

Teenage Call Girls

Give Back My Lover!

> **"While they're drinking themselves to death, let them have a cigarette. With the death penalty, you used to allow someone one last smoke."**
>
> California Attorney General Dan Lungren, on his state's new ban on smoking in bars

HEARTTHROB

Think of it as a love beeper (more than a million Japanese purchasers do). The little electronic gadget, which should be in the U.S. later this year, can be set to send a signal that you're looking for amour. If there's an appropriately gendered Lovegety in the neighborhood, set to the same signal, lights will flash and alarms will sound so that you can find each other. And then what? The instructions don't say.

A HUNGER FOR FOOTBALL?

As John Elway was leading the Broncos to victory at Super Bowl XXXII, the excitement caused a good many Americans to reach for the phone. To call mom? The bookie? Not exactly, as can be seen from the list at right.

BRINGING IT HOME

The five heaviest pizza-delivery days:

New Year's Day

Super Bowl Sunday

Thanksgiving eve

Halloween

New Year's Eve

GOLDEN OLDIES

Maturity was rewarded at the 40th annual Grammy Awards night. Bob Dylan (above), Elton John, Tony Bennett and John ("Sooner or later you become old enough to win a Grammy") Fogerty all took home honors. Song of the Year, though, went to relative spring chickens Shawn Colvin and John Leventhal for "Sunny Came Home."

> **"How can you write a history of the last seventy-five years and not talk about AIDS?"**
>
> Writer and gay activist Larry Kramer, chastising *Time*'s editors for not mentioning AIDS or gay rights in the magazine's 75th-anniversary issue

AMAZING GRACE

In January, *Today* cohost Katie Couric lost her husband, Jay Monahan, 42, to cancer. After a month at home with her two young daughters, Couric returned to the show on February 24. Her only reference to her own heartbreak included reaching out to others: "For all of you who may be struggling with a life-threatening disease right now and wondering how the world can keep doing business as usual, just know that my heart goes out to you."

DANCE WITH ME, BABY

After taking its first steps on the Internet, the new kid was ready for the big time: The computer-animated (and thus far gender-neutral) Dancing Baby made its first television appearance—on *Ally McBeal*—and the audience went wild. So did the marketers. Coming soon to a mall near you: some 70 baby cha-cha products.

THE POTOMAC WATCH

"We elected him President, not pope."
Clinton backer Barbra Streisand, on an alleged sexual relationship between the President and former White House intern Monica Lewinsky

"He has such a tremendous personality that I think the ladies just go wild over him."
Evangelist Billy Graham, on the same subject

"I'm staying the heck out of that."
Former President George Bush, on recent events in the capital

"I was under that very desk thirty-five years ago, and I could tell you there's barely room for a three-year-old."
John F. Kennedy Jr., on the difficulty of fooling around in the Oval Office

A SMALL DOSE OF HISTORY
The Post Office celebrated child labor reforms with a Lewis Hine photo of a young southern millworker and reminded us how much fun it is to draw outside the lines with a stamp commemorating the all-time favorite "school tool."

"You cannot strike your boss and still hold your job— unless you play in the NBA."
NBA commissioner David Stern, on the ruling to reinstate Latrell Sprewell's contract after his suspension for choking his coach last year

STARSHINE
Gloria Stuart, wearing the $20 million Winston Blue (white diamonds around a 15-carat blue diamond) necklace, was radiant on Oscar night. She was also, at 87, the oldest Best Supporting Actress nominee in the Academy's history.

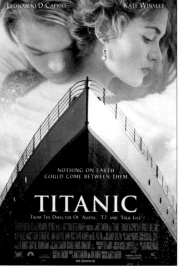

A NIGHT TO REMEMBER

Titanic tied *All About Eve* for most Academy Award nominations (14) and *Ben-Hur* for most wins (11). The wins:

Best Picture

Best Director

Art Direction

Cinematography

Sound

Sound Effects Editing

Original Dramatic Score

Original Song ("My Heart Will Go On")

Costume Design

Film Editing

Visual Effects

There were a few non-*Titanic* awards, including:

Best Actor—Jack Nicholson

Best Actress—Helen Hunt

Best Supporting Actor—Robin Williams

Best Supporting Actress—Kim Basinger

UNSINKABLE "TITANIC"

From its buoyancy at the box office, you'd never know that this ship went down. Can anyone remember now that the movie, with its staggering cost overruns, seemed headed for disaster? But it sailed straight into the record books: $1.8 billion in tickets, a $30 million sale to television, an expected $700 million in global video receipts, some $400 million in sales for the sound track album. And the wealth was spread around. Booksellers, auctioneers, video game makers—all got a slice of the biggest pie in movie history.

CHANTILLY LACE

The beaded dress that Rose almost took the plunge in was available through the J. Peterman catalog for a titanic $35,000.

A SWALLOWING SEA

The night the great ship went down, the crewmembers posted in the crow's nest to spot trouble had—unaccountably—not been issued binoculars.

KING OF THE WORLD?

He sure is. Director James Cameron not only made out like a bandit at the Academy Awards, he's also getting a handsome piece of *Titanic*'s profits. When all is calculated, his paycheck will be in the neighborhood of $150 million.

LEO! LEO! LEO!

Teenage fans everywhere wanted to bring cover guy of the year Leonardo DiCaprio home to mom. Mom would have been very, very grateful.

ALONE AT LAST!

Privacy was a precious commodity aboard the RMS *Titanic*, although some staterooms had private 50-foot promenades. There were more than 1,300 passengers, nearly 900 crew and staff.

THE OLYMP

Fire on the ice, grace in the air, ferocity on the slopes— America's female athletes came to conquer.

HEINZ KLUETMEIER
SPORTS ILLUSTRATED

IC WOMEN

Nailed it! Tara Lipinski
roars into Olympic history
as the youngest women's
figure-skating champion ever.

"All your life, you play hockey because you love it. Then you realize you're a girl."
—Cammi Granato

The snow never seemed to stop. The 14-hour time difference killed all suspense. A drug controversy embroiled the newly admitted snowboarding event. Could anything save this Olympics?

Enter the American women. Fresh-faced, fun and fearless, they arrived in Nagano thirsty for gold. Tara Lipinski reveled in the entire Olympic experience—marching in the opening ceremonies, posing with 516-pound sumo wrestler Akebono and bunking in the Olympic Village. Teammate Michelle Kwan (above, right) holed up in a hotel with her parents, and her caution didn't end there: "Michelle skated not to lose, and Tara skated to win," said their friend, skater Todd Eldredge. Lipinski displayed newly acquired artistry, twirling like a jewelry-box ballerina in her dazzling signature move—a triple loop–triple loop combination. When it was over, her upraised arms enfolded the cheering audience. The gold was hers. And Kwan's graciousness in accepting silver defined the Olympic ideal.

Theirs were not the only triumphs. Freestyle aerialist Nikki Stone (above, left) soared to first place, just two years after a "career-ending" back injury. As a child, Cammi Granato (center, at left) disguised herself by tucking her hair into her helmet so she could play the "boys only" sport. In the debut of women's hockey at the Olympics, Granato helmed a 3–1 victory against No. 1–seeded Canada. At the final buzzer, sticks and gloves sailed through the air and well-padded players heaped themselves onto their puck-eating goalie, Sarah Tueting, who had made a mind-boggling 21 saves. Chosen by the team captains of seven other sports to carry the American flag in the closing ceremonies, Granato said, "I'm really living out all my dreams."

With victory seconds away, goaltender Sarah Tueting leaps in elation. When Tueting was chosen over fellow netminder Sara DeCosta as the starting goalie, her rival responded by giving her a cherished lucky guardian angel pin. "A selfless act," says Tueting. "That's what our team is about."

Tara summed it up for comebackers and newcomers alike: "It felt so good, so perfect."

Picabo Street's own dream—of a comeback—appeared unattainable. Not only had the Lillehammer silver medalist ripped two knee ligaments 14 months before, but less than two weeks prior to the Olympics she had been knocked unconscious when she crashed in a Swedish race. Perhaps her New Age aura summoned the morning sun to slightly melt the Super G course for the competitors who followed her. After curving too wide at an early gate, the Bengal-helmeted Street turned on the power and hurtled down the mountain, letting "my skis take me through the finish line." She won by 1/100 of a second—the slimmest margin in Olympic history.

And that's what it came down to, after a lifetime of grueling training and sacrificed social events and obsessing and dreaming—a nanosecond, an imperceptible wobble, a flicker in concentration. That's what these mighty and marvelous women know and live with, and why, despite all of this year's Olympic problems, they prevailed.

Tiger, tiger, turning tight: Picabo Street slams down the Super G course at 80 mph.

SPRING

Hitting Her Stride

Accompanied by her bow-tied lawyer, William Ginsburg, a power-suited Monica Lewinsky left FBI offices in Los Angeles on May 28 after providing fingerprints and voice and handwriting samples. Less than a week later, the flamboyant Ginsburg was replaced by two attorneys gauged to be more politically savvy.

40

APR. 1 U.S. District Judge Susan Webber Wright dismisses Paula Jones's **sexual harassment lawsuit** against President Clinton. Jones claimed that in 1991 then-Governor Clinton asked her for oral sex in an Arkansas hotel room. Wright rules that the alleged behavior, while "boorish and offensive," is not legally actionable.

APR. 6 Citicorp and Travelers Group announce a partnership to create the largest financial-services conglomerate in the world. By day's end both companies' **stock has skyrocketed,** adding $14 billion to a deal already valued at $70 billion in stock—the world's largest merger to date. The new organization will be called Citigroup.

APR. 6 A study of 13,388 healthy women at high risk for breast cancer shows the drug tamoxifen reduced incidence of the disease by 45 percent. While medical experts hail tamoxifen as **a breakthrough in cancer prevention,** they also warn of grave side effects, including blood clots and increased risk of uterine cancer.

APR. 13 Dolly, the world's first cloned sheep, gives birth—the old-fashioned way—to a healthy 13-pound 2-ounce **baby lamb.** Daughter Bonnie's arrival proves Dolly can breed normally and produce healthy offspring, say scientists at Scotland's Roslin Institute.

Blood in the Street
Outrage over the deaths of six students— shot while protesting sky-high prices for fuel and electricity—exploded into riots in the Indonesian capital of Jakarta. An estimated 500 died during the three-day May rampage, many of them looters trapped in buildings torched by other rioters. Almost before the acrid smoke cleared, President Suharto had resigned.

43

APR. 19 China frees political prisoner Wang Dan, a student leader of the 1989 **Tiananmen Square** democracy movement, and flies him to the U.S. for "medical reasons." But his release is reportedly part of a deal negotiated with the Clinton administration to soften the U.S. stance on China's human rights policies.

APR. 20 Kenyan runner Moses Tanui, 32, **wins the Boston Marathon**—for the second time—in 2 hours 7 minutes 34 seconds, the third-fastest time in the history of the race.

APR. 24 ABC confirms it will cancel *Ellen*, the first television series to feature an openly gay lead character. More than 36 million people tuned in last year to watch Ellen's **"coming out,"** but ratings later plummeted. Other eponymous shows ending this season: CBS's *Murphy Brown* and *Cybill*.

Where Madness Dwelled

Now settled in the fluorescent glare of a Sacramento warehouse, this 11-by-13 shack once stood in a Montana forest and was home to ex-math professor Theodore Kaczynski. Before a flatbed truck took it away as trial evidence, authorities removed hundreds of books, tin cans, old diplomas and newspaper clippings, sleeping pills, three manual typewriters, and pipes and timing devices for building bombs like the ones that killed three people and injured 29. The confessed Unabomber now resides in a prison cell, sentenced in May to four life terms plus 30 years.

RICHARD BARNES

APR. 30 In a foreign-policy triumph for the beleaguered Clinton administration, the Senate votes overwhelmingly to **expand NATO** to include former iron curtain countries Poland, Hungary and the Czech Republic. The three nations will be formally admitted to NATO at a 50th anniversary summit next April.

APR. 30 During a live broadcast of Daniel Jones's standoff with police on a Los Angeles freeway, several local news channels and MSNBC **continue broadcasting** when Jones sets himself ablaze and shoots himself to death. Coverage of the gruesome suicide leads to outraged calls from viewers and inspires national debate over responsible journalism.

MAY 7 German carmaker Daimler-Benz buys the Chrysler Corp. for close to $40 billion, **the largest industrial merger** on record.

MAY 11 India detonates three underground nuclear devices in the northwestern desert, **violating a global ban** on nuclear testing. The blasts, which are more powerful than the atomic bomb dropped on Hiroshima, draw swift condemnation from around the globe and raise the specter of a nuclear arms race between India and its bitter rival, Pakistan.

Guarding a Treasure
During their June trip to China, the Clinton family mingled with terra-cotta sentries from an emperor's tomb. As the Lewinsky scandal unfolded in coming months, we grew to doubt the image of the happy family pictured here—with one exception: Chelsea. The Clintons' unwavering love and scrupulous protection of their poised, appealing 18-year-old daughter remained unquestioned.

47

MAY 13 Two days after its earlier tests, India sets off a **second round of nuclear blasts.** Prime Minister Atal Bihari Vajpayee maintains the tests are necessary for India's national security. But within hours the U.S. and Japan impose tough economic sanctions, including an end to all American aid except humanitarian assistance.

MAY 14 The last episode of *Seinfeld,* the wildly popular television series about four self-absorbed New Yorkers, is **watched by more than 76 million people.** The much-hyped finale of the show "about nothing" inspires bashes around the world (in Cannes, France, 500 people gather around giant outdoor monitors at three a.m. to catch it live) and entices advertisers to pay an estimated $1.7 million, unprecedented for a 30-second commercial.

MAY 18 The U.S. Department of Justice and 20 state attorneys general file sweeping **antitrust lawsuits** against Microsoft, which controls 90 percent of the software market. Both suits accuse Microsoft of using monopolistic practices.

License to Kill

James Byrd Jr., a former vacuum-cleaner salesman, was hitching a ride home after attending his niece's bridal shower. It is alleged that three white men stopped to offer Byrd, a black man, a lift; drove him to a secluded area; beat him up, then chained him to the back of this pickup truck and dragged him to his death. The three are charged with murder. The bloody two-mile stretch of east Texas back road seemed, for a time, to stretch across a stunned nation.

MAY 21 Kipland Kinkel, 15, shoots at students in his high school cafeteria in Springfield, Oreg., killing two and injuring 25. **The rampage ends** when several students, led by wounded varsity wrestler Jacob Ryker, tackle Kinkel. An hour later, police find Kinkel's parents, both teachers, shot dead in their home. The freshman is charged with four counts of murder.

MAY 28 A scientific team presents an image of what may be a new planet outside our solar system. Dr. Susan Terebey discovered the rogue planet— zooming away from its parent stars **at about 20,000 mph**—from digitized photographs taken by the Hubble Space Telescope last summer.

MAY 28 Pakistan explodes several nuclear devices near the Afghanistan border. "Today, **we have settled the score** with India," says Pakistani Prime Minister Nawaz Sharif, referring to India's tests earlier this month. The U.S., Japan and other nations respond with economic sanctions.

MAY 31 Singer Ginger Spice (Geri Halliwell), 25, shakes up the preteen universe when she bids farewell to the Spice Girls, the phenomenally lucrative British band, citing "differences between us." The remaining Spices—**Baby, Posh, Scary, Sporty**—say they'll finish their summer concert tour without her.

In Harm's Way

A deadly series of tornadoes with winds of 260 mph ripped a 22-mile swath through Alabama in early April. In hardest-hit Jefferson County, a twister smashed 443 houses into kindling. Dozens died, including a couple married nearly 70 years who were found together. Still, there were miracles. Near Birmingham worshipers huddled in a hall amid flying glass and debris as their church was torn apart. Two supporting walls held firm. Said one survivor: "God's hand just went in that hallway."

JUNE 2 Californians pass a ballot measure that will replace bilingual education in public schools with intensive one-year **English immersion classes.** Civil rights groups file suit the next day to overturn Proposition 227.

JUNE 3 In one of Germany's worst rail disasters, a train traveling at 125 mph **veers off the track** and crashes into a road bridge, which then topples onto several passenger cars. In all, 101 people are killed and 80 injured. Authorities suggest a broken wheel may have been the culprit.

JUNE 4 Terry Nichols is sentenced to **life in prison without parole** for conspiring with Timothy McVeigh to blow up the Oklahoma City Federal Building in 1995. The explosion killed 168 people.

JUNE 5 "Well, I'm still here," is 95-year-old Bob Hope's comeback to reports of his death, broadcast on C-SPAN just minutes earlier. Congressman Bob Stump had mistakenly **eulogized the comedian** on the House floor after an obituary appeared on the Associated Press Web site.

JUNE 8 Actor Charlton Heston is elected president of the National Rifle Association and vows **to lead the gun lobby** into "the mainstream."

Starvation in Sudan

As Sudan's civil war entered its 16th year, fighting intensified between the Islamic regime and rebels in the predominantly Christian south. So did the northern-based government's efforts to starve southern civilians into submission. By April, when diplomatic pressure forced the regime to lift restrictions on humanitarian aid flights (at right, villagers carry home donated food), 1.2 million people faced starvation. In July, the U.N. mounted its biggest air drop ever, but it was too late to save thousands.

ALESSANDRO ABBONIZIO
AFP

JUNE 9 The Southern Baptist Convention amends its statement of faith to include a short declaration on marriage that rankles feminists, many Baptist churches and some scholars. Conservative Southern Baptist leaders defend the declaration, including the statement " a wife is to **submit graciously** to the servant leadership of her husband," as a healing response to the disintegration of the American family.

JUNE 10 The Wisconsin Supreme Court rules that taxpayer money may be used for low-income students in Milwaukee to attend religious schools. In **a landmark decision,** the court argues that Milwaukee's voucher program, which allows disadvantaged children to attend private schools tuition-free, "has a secular purpose" and therefore doesn't breach the First Amendment's separation of church and state.

JUNE 11 Mitsubishi of America settles the largest sexual harassment case filed by the U.S. government. The automaker agrees to pay $34 million to end a federal lawsuit that claims hundreds of female employees had endured **groping and crude jokes from male workers** at its plant in Normal, Ill. Demonstrations and a boycott of Mitsubishi cars had spurred the company to settle private suits in 1997.

A Giant in Paris

Sixty-five-foot Ho, representing Asia, trundled across the Pont Neuf on forklift feet in the Paris parade that launched soccer's World Cup. In streets clogged with giddy celebrants, yellow-shirted Brazilians and kilt-wearing Scots snapped photos of one another, anticipating the kickoff match between their countries. Ho later met up with 42-ton brethren Moussa, Pablo and Romeo at the Place de la Concorde for an evening of spectacle. Their creator, Jean-Pascal Levy-Trumet, called them "ambassadors of the world population, reminders of fairy tales."

55

JUNE 17 Senate Republicans kill broad legislation designed to **curb teenage smoking.** The bill's death knell came this spring when cigarette companies launched an ad campaign portraying the bill as a Big Government ploy to "tax and spend." The tobacco industry had supported the legislation until Congress added costs and removed liability protection for the industry.

JUNE 18 *The Boston Globe* asks columnist and Pulitzer Prize finalist Patricia Smith, 42, to resign after she admits to **inventing people and quotes** in four recent columns. Smith, the first black female columnist on the *Globe* metro desk, had won a passionate following among readers.

JUNE 28 The *Cincinnati Enquirer* publishes a front-page apology and agrees to **pay more than $10 million** to Chiquita Brands International to halt a lawsuit over a May 3 exposé that accused the world's largest banana producer of unethical business practices. The newspaper capitulates after concluding that lead reporter Mike Gallagher had stolen 2,000 internal Chiquita voice mails, the content of which informed some of the article's allegations.

Summer and Smoke

Florida's "Holiday Fire" began on Memorial Day and had consumed 1,000 acres of wilderness in the Apalachicola National Forest by evening. Despite the best efforts of firefighters from all over the country— at right, Lorenzo Macias and Darren Davis of the California Hot Shots set backfires near Daytona Beach—more than 2,200 blazes turned the state into cinders over the next six weeks. In July, at last, the rains came.

TAKE YOUR MEDICINE

The butt of this year's bad jokes is a little pill for male potency: 1,152,430 of these were sold in the first week, and the Pentagon budgeted $50 million for Viagra. We'll leave the last word to Elizabeth Dole, whose husband, Bob, helped test it: "It is a great drug."

THE SPRING REPORT

APRIL MAY JUNE

Only the second quarter, and already we think of 1998 as the Year of El Niño. How can one "child" wreak so much devastation? But there is another sort of devastation in store, a literal blast from an unexpected arena: India and Pakistan flex their muscles at each other in a dangerous revival of the nuclear arms race. In Washington, D.C., Independent Counsel Kenneth Starr is flexing too, calling a parade of witnesses before a grand jury. They include President Clinton's advisers, his personal secretary and his friend Vernon Jordan. There is also a friend of Monica Lewinsky's. Her name is Linda Tripp, and as it turns out, she is no friend.

> "Don't confuse having
> a career with having a life.
> They are not the same."

Commencement speaker Hillary
Clinton, at Howard University

RATING ROSEBUD

The American Film Institute provoked
us all—quite deliberately—by naming
the 100 "best" American movies. *Citizen
Kane* headed the list, with *Casablanca*
at No. 2. But even the bottom of the
list was impressive: James Cagney's
stellar turn as George M. Cohan, the
Yankee Doodle Dandy.

HELLO AGAIN

The Chicago Bulls won their sixth NBA
title in eight seasons in an 87–86
thriller against the Utah Jazz. Michael
Jordan, unstoppable yet again, was
named the series MVP for a sixth time.

> "I tell you, that Michael Jackson
> is unbelievable, isn't he? Three
> plays in twenty seconds!"

Vice President Gore, on Michael Jordan's
impressive play in the NBA finals

A ROARING SUCCESS

The Lion King took its proper
share of Broadway's Tony awards:
six in all, including Best Musical.
Art was pronounced Best Play; *The
Beauty Queen of Leenane*, *Cabaret*
and *Ragtime* each won four awards.

"Spice Girls are way stupid, and I like them."

Zoya Gleizer of Washington, D.C., reacting to the retirement of Ginger Spice from the Spice Girls

"Hope they go defunct. My eleven-year-old thinks it's normal to strut around half-naked. At least Celine Dion has talent and gets dressed."

Jo-Ann Moss of West Linn, Oreg., on the same subject

THE ROARING '20s

The new Post Office stamps give us a history lesson: Federal agents poured illegal wine away, but they couldn't stop the flapper-fueled Charleston era that it gave rise to.

"He won't forget it. He'll think about it every day, like I do."

Don Larsen, former New York Yankees pitcher, and the only other person to pitch a perfect game at Yankee Stadium, on David Wells's May 17 game

AND THEN HE KISSED ME
Luciano Pavarotti, the largest of the tenor trio, planted big wet ones on the Ginger-less Spice Girls quartet after a benefit concert for children in Italy.

HOT WHEELS
Before cycling became a sport, it was biking, and it was fun. One reason was the Apple Krate bike, first made 30 years ago. Production ended in 1973, but the muscular former star of Schwinn's Sting-Ray line is back this year, banana seat and all (so you can still give your buddies a totally illegal ride on the back).

AM I BLUE?
It's quite small and very energetic and goes like the wind. Tara Lipinski? No, it's iMac, the cuddly computer from Apple. With a modest price tag and only three basic parts, the iMac finally makes sense of the phrase "user friendly."

"What's recess?"

A kindergartner, Toya Gray, at an Atlanta school where recess has been abolished

CHICKEN SOUP FOR THE WALLET

First you get turned down by 33 publishers. Then you find a small company that will print a few copies of your book. Then, if you're the authors of *Chicken Soup for the Soul,* you build a series and sell more than 28 million copies. During one June week, five of the top 10 paperback books on the best-seller list of the trade journal *Publishers Weekly* had *Chicken Soup* titles.

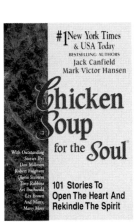

PRIDE OF THE PARROT HEADS

In June, Jimmy Buffett's memoir, *A Pirate Looks at Fifty,* went straight to No. 1. His *Where Is Joe Merchant?* was on the fiction list in 1992. Only five other authors have had best-sellers on both the fiction and nonfiction book lists: Ernest Hemingway, Dr. Seuss, John Steinbeck, William Styron and Irving Wallace. None of those guys had platinum records—or fans like these.

TINKY WINKY, LAA-LAA, DIPSY AND PO

If you see a purple dinosaur carrying an UNFAIR TO BARNEY sign, blame it on the Teletubbies. Debuting on American TV in April, Britain's new Fab Four is aimed specifically, and mesmerizingly, at toddlers. From the group's hit single, "Say Eh-Oh," you'd never know that one of its creators is a speech therapist.

THE POTOMAC WATCH

"I want you to know that the office of independent counsel can indict my dog. They can indict my cat. But I'm not going to lie about the President."

Former Clinton confidant Webster Hubbell

"The outrage of the American people toward the peccadilloes of their politicians is inversely proportional to the state of the economy."

Former Senate Ethics Committee chairman Warren Rudman

"He asked if it was an April Fools' joke."

Mike McCurry, White House press secretary, on the President's reaction to the news that Paula Jones's suit had been dismissed

"I have not come this far to see the law let men who have done such things dodge their responsibility."

Paula Jones, on her decision to appeal the dismissal of her lawsuit

50: BIRTH OF A NATION

On May 14, 1948, the sovereign state of Israel came into being and offered a homeland to survivors of the Holocaust.

150 YEARS AGO: OUR FOREMOTHERS

Elizabeth Cady Stanton and Lucretia Mott conceived the women's rights convention that was held in 1848 in Seneca Falls, N.Y. Delegates pressed for the vote for women, thereby sparking great ridicule.

200: SEND IN THE MARINES

A 1798 act of Congress called for a "drum major, fife major, and 32 drums and fifes." The United States Marine Band has evolved but is still, as it was 200 years ago, "The President's Own."

HAPPY ANNIVERSARY!

In 1778, King Louis XVI of France declared war on the British in support of American rebels. In 1868, impeached President Andrew Johnson was acquitted in the Senate by one vote. One hundred twenty-five years ago, a stunned world witnessed the birth of . . . oleomargarine. Marking anniversaries celebrates the past in a spirit that reflects the meaning of the event: philosophical, political, passionate, casual. There is room here for matters of great moment, but also room to note that the former Soviet Union held its first beauty contest just 10 years ago.

20: TRICK OR TREAT

Jamie Lee Curtis found herself in a near-terminal pickle in 1978's *Halloween*, and had so much fun she did it again this year, in *Halloween: H20*. Her play-it-straight bravado almost makes the splatter-screamer genre seem respectable. Almost.

40: ELVIS SIGHTING

Millions wept as Private Presley hoisted his duffel bag and joined other inductees at Fort Chaffee, Ark. That was 40 years ago, and some are still weeping!

125: BARELY BROKEN IN

Levi Strauss got the patent for putting rivets in work pants in 1873, but he'd been making "duck-waist overalls" like these for several years.

25: A FALL FROM GRACE; A CORONATION

In 1973, President Nixon addressed the nation as the Watergate scandal—which would lead to his resignation under threat of impeachment—rocked the country. That same year, one of the most impressive athletes of all time, Secretariat (a.k.a. Big Red), won horse racing's Triple Crown.

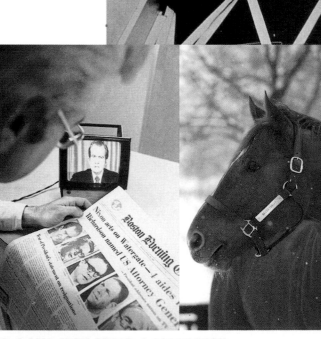

50: THE EARLY NEWS

CBS is 50 this year, and so is its news broadcasting. Before special effects, before CNN, before the Internet, there was Douglas Edwards with his up-to-the-minute visual aids.

THAT GLORIOUS YEAR

It was a rare gem of a season on the diamond.

Back when baseball scheduled doubleheaders, the great Ernie Banks used to stroll onto the grass, declare the weather beautiful and suggest, "Let's play two." He was a Chicago Cub when all games at Wrigley Field were played during the day. They play some at night there now, under the lights. But when young Kerry Wood, a classic hoss of a pitcher, took the mound for the Cubbies, you swore you were back in the days of doubleheaders.

65

"Best season ever," said Montreal manager Felipe Alou. "The game has emerged from the grave with thunder."

"The idol of today pushes the hero of yesterday out of our recollection," wrote Washington Irving in *The Sketch Book.* A nice little homily, but baseball proves it false. When we look upon the magnificent 1998 season, we see not only the idols of today but, more vividly than at any time in recent years, the heroes of yesterday. Mark McGwire didn't bury Roger Maris and Babe Ruth; he resurrected them. We watched the old clips once more. We saw the Maris boys, spitting images of their dad, being bear-hugged by this beast who had just shattered their old man's mark. It was sweet and sentimental, a peanuts-and–Cracker Jack moment.

It happened all around the diamond. The champion Yankees were so good they rekindled a smoldering debate: Which was the best team ever? Suddenly the 1927 and '39 Yanks, the '54 Indians and Cincinnati's Big Red Machine of the mid-'70s were alive again. In the American League, no one could figure out who was a better shortstop: Nomar Garciaparra of Boston, Derek Jeter of New York or Seattle's Alex Rodriguez. The only consensus: There hadn't been three more sensational players at the same position since Mickey Mantle, Willie Mays and Duke Snider patrolled the outfield simultaneously on different New York City ballfields.

Roger Clemens won his fifth Cy Young Award—no one had ever done that before—and the big righthander reminded us of past fireballers named Seaver and Gibson and Feller and Walter

It was a season of thrilling stories. Just 10 months after fleeing his native Cuba, Orlando Hernández (opposite, far left) was pitching in the World Series for the mighty Yankees. Just moments after watching their Padres lose to the Yankees in that Series, bleacherites in San Diego (center) forced their hobbled hero, Tony Gwynn, to take a curtain call. Before, during and after their titanic home-run duel, Sammy Sosa and Mark McGwire (near left) behaved like the classiest of competitors while evolving into the best of friends. All year long, youngsters like Garciaparra (this page) dazzled, leaving fans marveling at the season, as McGwire himself did after hitting his 70th, "It's absolutely amazing. It blows me away."

Like the Jack Armstrong
heroes of yore, he soldiered
on in 2,632 straight games,
then sat himself down. Next
night, Cal Ripken Jr. was, of
course, back at third. Ripken
is of the future, too: His record
may be the one mark that
lasts forever, and the man
himself will play again in
'99. His current streak is
seven games.

St. Louis outfielder Ray Lankford said the season was "baseball the way it used to be, like when we were kids."

"Big Train" Johnson. "The Rocket's a throwback," they said of
Clemens. Meantime, Kerry Wood of the Chicago Cubs struck out
20 in a game, something that had previously been accomplished
only by Roger Clemens. Wood reminded us that there are throwbacks-
in-waiting.

The idol of today, Irving continued, "will, in turn, be
supplanted by his successor of tomorrow." No he won't, not in baseball.
His records will be broken, sure—they were made to be. But will
Kerry Wood make us forget Roger Clemens? Could we ever possibly
forget the image—the 70 images—of McGwire crushing the ball?
Unthinkable. In baseball, when the game is great—and it was great
this year—the present is always the past, and so is the future.

68

SUMMER

Shootout on the Hill

On a sultry July afternoon, the cool marble hallway of the Capitol Building echoed with the crack of gunfire. Screaming tourists dove for cover and a Capitol police officer in the Great Rotunda raced for the stairs after a deranged gunman barged through a security checkpoint. When it was over, two officers lay dead in "the people's house," democracy's symbol.

70

JULY 2 CNN and *Time* retract a story, aired last month on CNN and published in *Time,* that charged the U.S. military used lethal nerve gas in a 1970 covert mission, called **Operation Tailwind,** in an attempt to kill American defectors in Laos. After separate investigations, each news organization concludes that evidence does not support the reporters' allegations.

JULY 5 Tennis player Pete Sampras, 26, defeats Croatian Goran Ivanisevic, 26, in five grueling sets to win his **fifth Wimbledon** and 11th Grand Slam championship. A day earlier, an overjoyed Jana Novotna, 29, of the Czech Republic, won her first Wimbledon title, beating Nathalie Tauziat, 30, of France.

JULY 7 Jailed Nigerian opposition leader Moshood K.O. Abiola, 60, dies of a heart attack shortly before his expected release. Many Nigerians considered Abiola their country's best hope for a **peaceful transition to democracy,** and his sudden death provokes riots that lead to more than 50 deaths by week's end, according to local newspapers.

A Wing and a Prayer

The day after this Boeing 747 made its roof-skimming, thrill-ride approach to Hong Kong's antiquated Kai Tak Airport, the vaunted new Chek Lap Kok Airport opened. The state-of-the-art facility, set on a 3,082-acre landfill, boasts an 88-gate terminal nearly a mile long. But the $20 billion price tag didn't avert a bumpy takeoff: Passengers were hampered by lost suitcases, blank flight information boards and malfunctioning escalators. Then computer glitches forced the city's major cargo company to temporarily transfer business back to shabby little Kai Tak.

73

JULY 9 Former high school couple Amy Grossberg, 19, and Brian Peterson, 20, are **sent to prison** for contributing to the death of their newborn child. Grossberg is sentenced to 30 months and Peterson, who cooperated with investigators, to 24 months. The infant was discovered in a garbage bin behind a Newark, N.J., motel in 1996.

JULY 10 The U.S. military delivers the remains of Air Force 1st Lt. Michael Blassie, the **Vietnam soldier** interred in Arlington Cemetery's Tomb of the Unknowns since 1984, to his family for reburial in St. Louis. Blassie's identity was confirmed by DNA tests in June.

JULY 12 Before dawn, arsonists throw a gasoline bomb into the home of Christine Quinn, a Roman Catholic, **killing her sleeping sons**—Richard, 10, Mark, nine, and Jason, seven. This attack in Ballymoney, Northern Ireland, occurs after a week of Protestant violence over the banning of an annual Protestant march through a nearby Catholic town.

Terror in Africa

A truck bomb exploded behind Nairobi's American embassy, hurling debris onto a flaming Haile Selassie Avenue and incinerating passengers in nearby buses. Amid the carnage and chaos, a crowd pulled this wounded man to a waiting ambulance. Within minutes of the first blast, another bomb went off 425 miles away at the American embassy in Tanzania. The coordinated terrorist attacks killed 224 and injured thousands; officials believe they were masterminded by Osama bin Laden, a wealthy Saudi exile and Islamic militant.

GILBERT OTIENO
SIPA PRESS

JULY 12 France's stunning 3–0 victory over Brazil in soccer's World Cup finals draws a television audience of about 1.7 billion people—roughly **a third of the earth's population** and 12 times the number of Americans who watched the Super Bowl this winter. In all, 704 players on 32 teams competed in France '98.

JULY 13 A video documentary of Abraham **Zapruder's home movie** of President John F. Kennedy's assassination in Dallas goes on sale for $19.98. Within two weeks, about 300,000 copies of *Image of an Assassination* will have been shipped to stores across the country.

JULY 17 A powerful undersea earthquake triggers a 23-foot wave that **sweeps away entire villages** in Papua New Guinea. Eight days later, the government reports 1,500 islanders are dead, 2,000 missing and thousands homeless.

A Married Man

During his four-decade struggle— more than half of it spent in prison—to overthrow apartheid, Nelson Mandela had little time for a personal life. His marriage to second wife Winnie ended bitterly in 1996. But in August, South Africa's first black president gave connubiality another try. At his 80th birthday party, he disclosed his wedding the previous day to human-rights campaigner Graça Machel, 52, widow of Mozambique's President Samora Machel. "Now you won't shout at me," said Mandela to Archbishop Desmond Tutu, who had long urged the lovers to legalize their union.

JULY 21 Chinese gymnast Sang Lan, 17, is paralyzed after a fall while practicing for the **women's vault competition** at the Goodwill Games in New York. A lengthy operation on Lan's spinal cord four days later fails to restore sensation below her upper chest.

JULY 23 A devastating heat wave—it has claimed more than 100 lives—has scorched the southern and southwestern U.S. since early summer, prompting President Clinton to designate **$100 million in federal aid** to help poor families in 11 states buy air conditioners and pay electric bills. He also declares the state of Texas a disaster area.

JULY 25 President Clinton is subpoenaed to appear before a federal grand jury regarding the Monica Lewinsky investigation. Independent Counsel Kenneth Starr **withdraws the subpoena** four days later, after Clinton agrees to give videotaped testimony at the White House with his lawyers present.

JULY 28 Independent Counsel Starr grants Monica Lewinsky, 25, blanket immunity from prosecution in return for Lewinsky's **"full and truthful testimony"** about her relationship with the President. The Starr-Lewinsky deal comes after six months of stormy negotiations.

May the Road Rise Up

Three Irish schoolboys who played together were buried side by side, innocents killed in Northern Ireland's worst terrorist attack ever. James and Shaun, both 12, and Oran, eight, had eagerly anticipated showing the market town of Omagh to a Spanish exchange student and teacher, also among the 29 who died when a 500-pound car bomb exploded. Wreaths atop the small coffins were in the colors of soccer teams beloved by the young fans. In his homily, the village priest asked, "Is this our saddest moment, our darkest hour? If it is, then will it herald a new dawn?"

IAN WALDIE
REUTERS-ARCHIVE PHOTOS

JULY 28 Serbian military forces seize the Kosovo town of Malisevo, concluding **a massive offensive** to wrest portions of the embattled province from ethnic Albanian rebels. The day before, tens of thousands of ethnic Albanians had fled as the Serbian troops advanced on Malisevo.

JULY 29 The United Auto Workers union ends a 54-day strike against General Motors. The strike cost GM about $2.8 billion in revenues, causing the company to slip behind Ford as the nation's top auto seller for the first time in nearly 30 years. Plant workers' lost wages amounted to about $1 billion. **"Nobody really won,** when you think about it," says UAW president Steve Yokich.

JULY 30 A group of Ohio machine-shop workers who call themselves **the Lucky 13** find out they've won the $295.7 million Powerball jackpot, the biggest-ever American lottery.

A Battle Over Bones

As Israel turned 50, the celebrations were almost drowned out by the squabbles—not just between Jews and Arabs, but also between religious Jews and their more secularized brethren. Skirmishes flared up in Jerusalem after archaeologists began exhuming bones from a 5th century cemetery that lay in the path of road builders. Although experts identified the tombs as Christian, ultra-Orthodox Jews believed the excavation was desecrating Jewish graves. On August 12, protesters clashed with authorities (left); elsewhere 200 militants stormed the construction site, vandalizing tractors and shouting "Nazis" at archaeologists and police. The cops won that battle, but the culture war continued to escalate.

DAOUD MIZRAHI
AFP

AUG. 6 During all-day testimony before a federal grand jury, Monica Lewinsky admits to **several sexual encounters** with President Clinton inside the White House. This account contradicts Lewinsky's previous sworn statement and the President's testimony in the Paula Jones case.

AUG. 9 Two Chicago boys, ages seven and eight, are charged with the murder of Ryan Harris, 11, whose badly beaten body was found in a vacant lot on July 28. The youth of the alleged offenders **shocks the nation**—but within three weeks, murder charges are dropped; soon afterward an adult is named as chief suspect.

AUG. 17 Hours after testifying before a federal grand jury, President Clinton tells the American people he had a relationship with Monica Lewinsky that was **"not appropriate."** To the dismay of his advisers, the President also attacks the Starr investigation during the four-minute speech.

Role Call

After a push from the U.S. Supreme Court, Virginia Military Institute admitted women in 1997 (22 survived that first year). This year, 34 female freshmen (or "rats"), including Tiffany Richards from Travis Air Force Base in California, lined up for another round of abuse. Cold comfort, but males will fare just as badly on the ratline as females, enduring six months of relentless ego-busting taunts, drills and calisthenics.

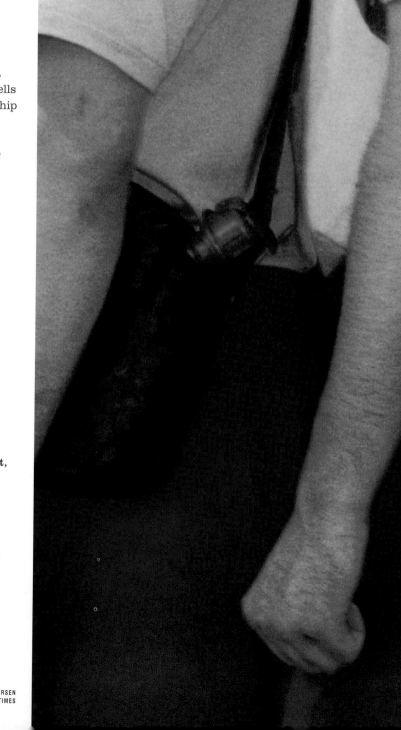

DON PETERSEN
THE ROANOKE TIMES

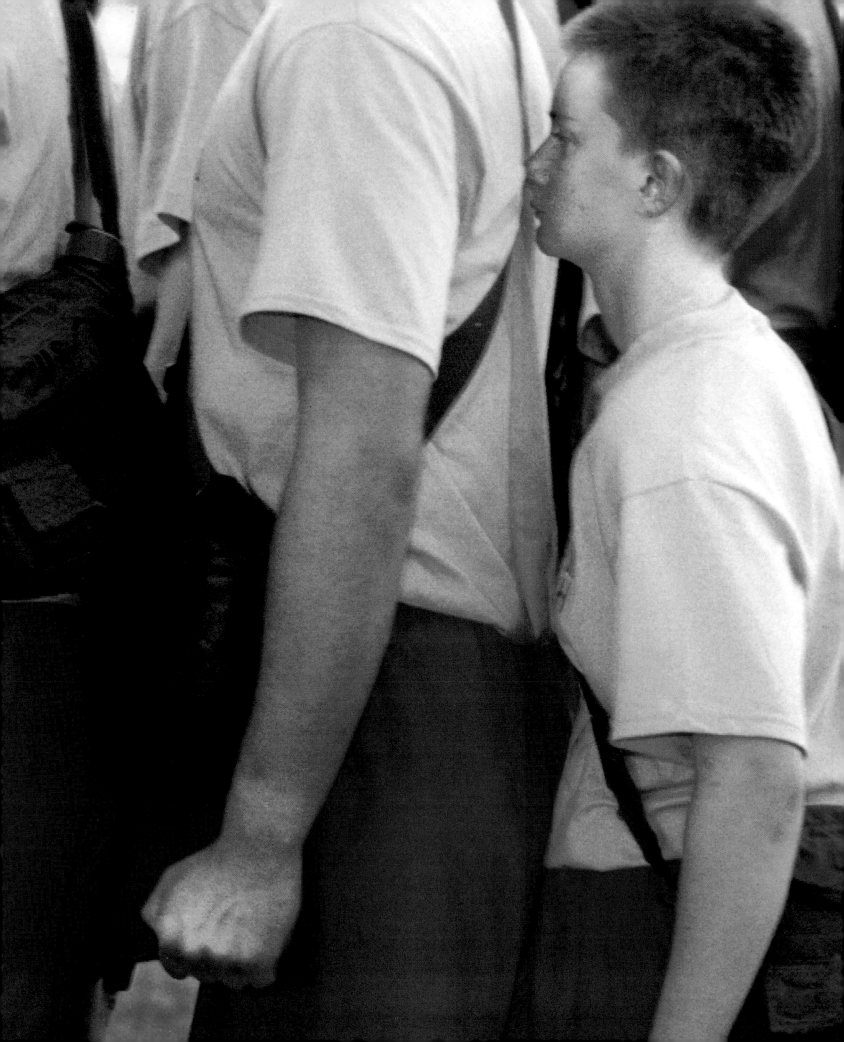

AUG. 19 *Boston Globe* columnist Mike Barnicle, 54, resigns amid allegations that he fabricated a 1995 column about two cancer victims. Earlier this month, the newspaper suspended him based on accusations that **he had plagiarized jokes** from comedian George Carlin. This episode follows on the heels of the *Globe*'s dismissal of Patricia Smith, another popular and controversial columnist.

AUG. 20 American cruise missiles demolish alleged terrorist training camps in Afghanistan and a chemical plant in Sudan suspected of manufacturing a lethal nerve gas. The White House defends the surprise attacks as **retribution for the recent American embassy bombings** in Kenya and Tanzania and as an offensive against the "imminent threat" of terrorism.

AUG. 21 Samuel Bowers, 73, a former imperial wizard of the Mississippi Ku Klux Klan, is **convicted of murder and sentenced to life** in prison for ordering the slaying of black civil rights activist Vernon Dahmer Sr. in 1966. Three juries had been deadlocked and unable to convict Bowers in previous trials during the 1960s.

Surge Protectors

Torrential floods, exacerbated by El Niño and unrestrained logging that has left denuded hills unable to absorb rain, inundated China. Three thousand life-jacketed soldiers in Harbin sang songs about courage before using sandbags and washbasins to hold back the raging Songhua River. These widely televised efforts, shown shortly after China's president accused the army of "rampant smuggling," also shored up the military's image.

85

WANG JIANMIN
CHINA FEATURES-SYGMA

AUG. 27 Chaos in Russia's economy sparks a global selling frenzy among stock market investors. **Markets tumble** in Japan, Europe, Mexico, Brazil and the U.S., where the Dow-Jones industrial average loses 357 points, or more than an estimated $400 billion in value. The following Monday, the Dow will plunge another 513 points—the second-steepest drop in its history—but then rally halfway back the next day.

AUG. 29 Little Leaguers from Toms River, N.J., **capture the World Series** title in Williamsport, Pa., by defeating a team from Kashima, Japan. About 2,000 friends and relatives greet the boys in an exuberant homecoming the next day.

SEPT. 1 Final DNA tests confirm that two Virginia toddlers, Callie Conley and Rebecca Chittum, both three, were **accidentally switched at birth** and sent home with the wrong parents in 1995. One of the children has already been orphaned by a Fourth of July car wreck and is living with her grandparents. The two families decide to keep the children they've raised and share visitation rights.

Unending Hunger
In August the U.N. airlifted 18,500 tons of food to southern Sudan. But getting it to those in need was another matter. Fighting between southern rebel factions in Sudan's civil war made aid distribution impossible in parts of the famine zone. And despite a humanitarian cease-fire in Bahr El Ghazal province, one of the hardest-hit areas, feeding centers (like this one in the town of Ajiep) could barely keep up with demand.

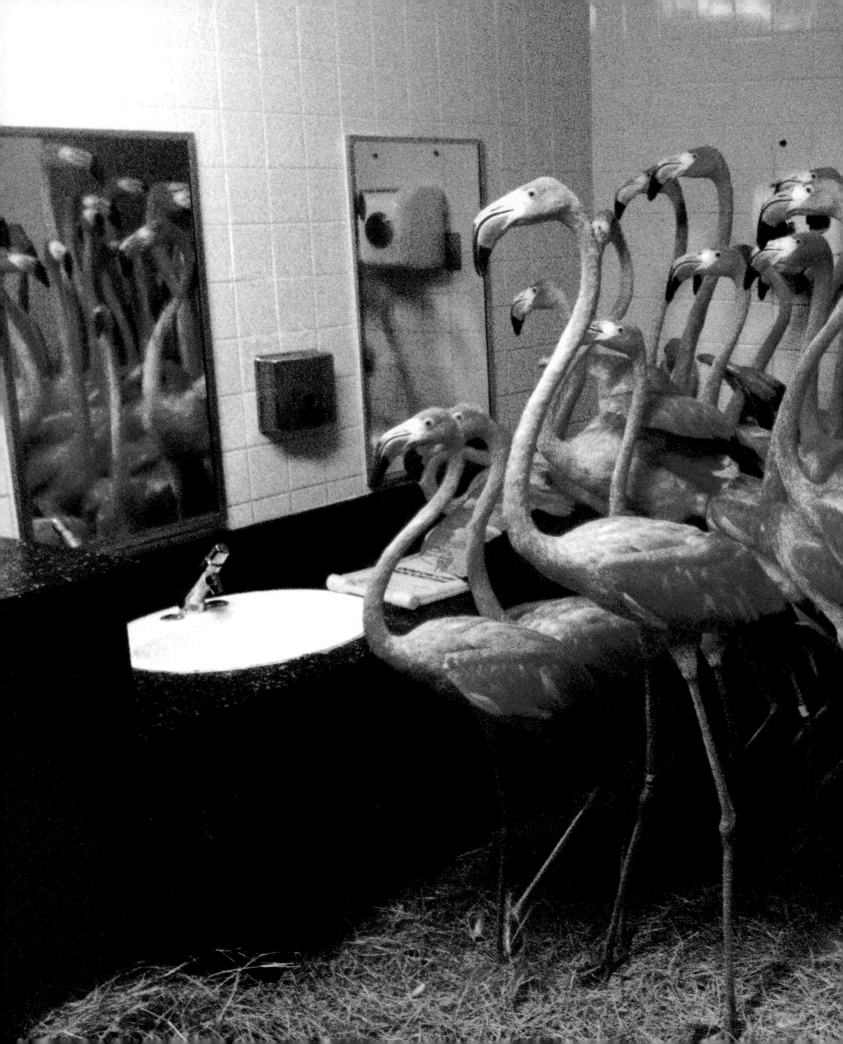

SEPT. 8 The Real IRA, a faction of the Irish Republican Army, **declares a cease-fire.** British and Irish leaders greet the announcement with cautious optimism.

SEPT. 9 The board of Manchester United, Britain's wealthiest soccer club, agrees to sell the team to **Rupert Murdoch's pay television network** for a record $1.03 billion.

SEPT. 10 An Air Force cargo plane returns Keiko, star of the movie *Free Willy,* to his native Icelandic waters in the first attempt ever to reintroduce a captive killer whale to the wild. **Keiko's odyssey** began five years ago when LIFE reported on the beloved orca's grim existence at a Mexican amusement park.

SEPT. 11 Millions of people flood the Internet to read the independent counsel's account of President Clinton's alleged wrongdoing. **The 445-page Starr report** accuses the President of 11 possibly impeachable offenses related to the Monica Lewinsky affair. The report fails to mention Whitewater or the other scandals that consumed the bulk of Starr's four-year, $40 million investigation.

In the Pink

Talk about pecking order. When Miami's Metrozoo moved animals indoors as a precaution against Hurricane Georges, a lemur got an office of its own, but these Caribbean flamingos wound up in the men's room. Turns out, with mirrors and, yes, available water and nothing to entangle their stilt legs, it's an ideal bird bunker. To get them there, Ron Magill, a staff zoologist, cornered the honking herd and grabbed them as they tried to fly past. "I just wrapped my arms around as many as I could," he said. His record is six at a time, quite a flamingo load.

89

DANIEL LECLAIRE
REUTERS-ARCHIVE PHOTOS

SEPT. 13 Patrick Rafter, 25, successfully defends his **U.S. Open men's title** against fellow Aussie Mark Philippoussis, 21. One day earlier, California's Lindsay Davenport, 22, had clinched the women's title by defeating top-ranked Martina Hingis, 17.

SEPT. 14 The Internal Revenue Service reports a dozen of its **top executives have been reprimanded** and another 132 workers face investigation following an outside review of reams of IRS records. The review panel uncovered instances of IRS managers setting collection quotas and evaluating employees based on enforcement actions taken against taxpayers.

SEPT. 15 Scientists report that **Jupiter's faint rings** are composed of dust from nearby moons, a finding that may help to resolve other mysteries about the formation of the solar system.

SEPT. 20 Cal Ripken Jr., 38, pulls himself out of the Baltimore Orioles lineup after playing 2,632 consecutive games over 16 years. In 1995, when **he eclipsed Lou Gehrig's record** of 2,130 games, Ripken thrilled the nation—and restored some joy to baseball, which was reeling from the players' strike that canceled the '94 World Series.

Tale of the Tape

Has any Hollywood star been more scrutinized than President Clinton when his four-hour, previously videotaped grand jury testimony aired in September? Alternately as steely-eyed as Clint Eastwood, as genial as Mister Rogers and as evasive as Michael Douglas in *Fatal Attraction*, the President transfixed the nation, including Carnegie Mellon graduate student Joe Ferris, as he admitted to "inappropriate, intimate contact" with Monica Lewinsky. Despite early reports that he was agitated and volatile, there wasn't a hint of performance anxiety.

JOHN BEALE
PITTSBURGH POST-GAZETTE

RAND JURY TESTIMONY

LIVE-TAPE FEED
FROM CONGRESS

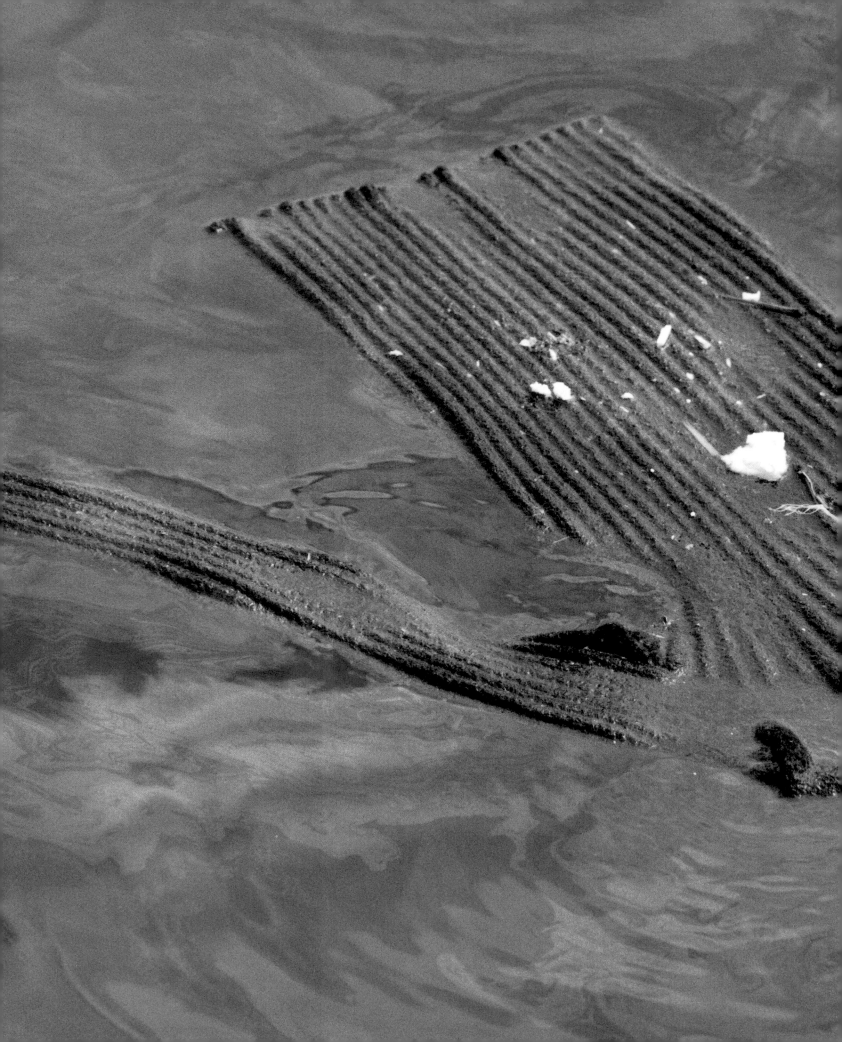

SEPT. 21 A jury orders psychiatrist Myron Liptzin to pay $500,000 in damages to Wendell Williamson, 30, a former patient who went on a deadly shooting spree in North Carolina eight months after leaving Liptzin's care. Williamson's lawyer argued that Liptzin was negligent for **not correctly diagnosing** Williamson as a paranoid schizophrenic, for not apprising him of the gravity of his condition and for not arranging for follow-up care.

SEPT. 22 Britain restores full diplomatic relations with Iran two days after President Mohammad Khatami tells journalists his government will not enforce Ayatollah Khomeini's 1989 **death edict against novelist Salman Rushdie.** Sadly for Rushdie, this announcement riles Iranian hard-liners who declare the *fatwa* can't be revoked and, several weeks later, raise the bounty on Rushdie to $2.8 million.

SEPT. 25 The FDA approves the drug Herceptin, a genetically engineered antibody that **slows the spread of metastatic breast cancer** in some of the women whose tumors overproduce the HER2 gene. Because Herceptin specifically targets malignant cells, it doesn't have the severe side effects of chemotherapy.

Lost at Sea

"Not one bit of hope," said a despairing fisherman, among the first to search a wreckage-filled sea off tiny Peggy's Cove, Nova Scotia. Sixteen minutes after Geneva-bound Swissair Flight 111 reported smoke in the cockpit, the jetliner crashed off the Canadian coast, killing all 229 aboard. "Although I never knew you, I shed tears for you," read a card attached to a bouquet of wildflowers, among the many left at the village lighthouse.

SANDOR FIZLI
HALIFAX DAILY NEWS-SIPA PRESS

SEPT. 27 In German elections, Gerhard Schroeder, 54, ousts Chancellor Helmut Kohl, the country's leader for 16 years. Schroeder's Social Democrats and the environmentalist Green Party also win majority seats in Parliament, signaling **a radical shift** from Kohl conservatism to an experimental, leftist government.

SEPT. 30 President Clinton announces the largest surplus in the federal budget in U.S. history—about $70 billion. As Democrats and Republicans **scramble to take credit** for the huge windfall, analysts ponder contributing factors, notably lower interest rates, a robust economy, the stock market's spectacular bull run and some very fancy accounting.

SEPT. 30 The Assassination Records Review Board issues a lengthy report on the murder of John F. Kennedy. During its six-year investigation, the board procured more than 60,000 documents from the FBI, CIA and other sources. It concludes that the government **"needlessly and wastefully classified"** important records, unnecessarily arousing suspicion among the American public.

Homer Odyssey

In baseball's forest of numbers, a few stats loom like sequoias. Babe Ruth's 1927 season total of 60 home runs stood unmatched for 34 years before Roger Maris launched 61. Then came the amazing summer of 1998, when two megasluggers vied to outdo Maris (and distract a grateful nation from Monicagate). On September 8, the Cardinals' Mark McGwire shattered the record and then traded hugs with archrival Sammy Sosa—fielding for the Cubs—after his victory lap. Big Mac ended the season with 70, making even redwoods look small.

ED REINKE
ASSOCIATED PRESS

STANDING TALL

Skirt slits went up, up, up.
Shirts became transparent.
Lingerie went from underwear
to outerwear. Any other skin
that could be showing? And
that's when the backs came
off the shoes.

THE SUMMER REPORT

JULY AUGUST SEPTEMBER

Although the weather was clearly one of the season's dominant themes, the media seemed incapable of covering anything but the swirl of scandal in our nation's capital. Old hostilities abroad surfaced again in Ireland, Israel and the fragments of the former Yugoslavia. No matter, we've got Monica. Kenneth Starr and his team, having quizzed their witnesses and formed their conclusions, wrote it all up and shared it with us: 18 boxes of backup material and a 445-page monument to banality and poor taste. After a quick surge of interest, most of America seemed ready, even anxious, to move on.

"PRACTICE" MAKES PERFECT

When Camryn Manheim of *The Practice* picked up her Emmy for Best Supporting Actress in a Drama Series, she accepted, gleefully, "for all the fat girls." A suggested revision: for all the great-looking big women with the courage to get out there and do wonderful work.

"I've never had champagne before."

Slugger Sammy Sosa, after the Cubs made the playoffs

"What's a Muppet?"

Majority leader of the House, Dick Armey, after hearing Newt Gingrich complain about a Muppet that was shown smoking a cigar

A NEW WOMAN

It's been a long, strange road for Paula Jones, and she's made a pit stop or two along the way: getting a new 'do, braces on her teeth, wardrobe tips and a new adviser, even (this summer) plastic surgery on her nose. That last visit, financed with $9,000 from an anonymous donor, was—for now— the finishing touch in the makeover.

"The kids are excited; they're like, 'Dad, let's *do* stuff!'"

Former NFL quarterback Boomer Esiason, who gets to see more of his family now that he's a commentator instead of a football player

HOT WHEELS

The prestigious Guggenheim Museum in New York City mounted an exhibit of more than 100 motorcycles. Reaching out to the tattoo-and-leather crowd? No, say the curators: These hogs embody important 20th century themes like technology, speed, rebellion and transformation. Besides, one critic added, "not every good show has to feel like eating your lima beans."

> "I had waterfront property, waterback property, waterside property, watereverywhere property."
>
> Jayne Howell, of Pascagoula, Miss., whose house was swamped by Hurricane Georges

MIXING IT UP

The Post Office makes strange bedfellows: Margaret Bourke-White, who changed American photography, and the streamlined appliances of the 1930s, which changed the American kitchen.

SYNCH OR SWIM

American Bill May, the first man to be on a synchronized swim team (with Kristina Lum, above), picked up two silver medals at the Goodwill Games. But the Amateur Swimming Union of the Americas later grumpily ruled against males in synchronized swimming events under its jurisdiction, so May won't get to compete in the 1999 Pan American Games.

> "The illusion of arms control is more dangerous than no arms control at all."
>
> U.N. weapons inspector Scott Ritter, resigning from his duties to protest U.S. and U.N. inaction in Iraq

SOMETHING HE ATE?

For a rollicking good time, it's Scotland in August. This gentleman attended Edinburgh's Fringe Festival, a guaranteed sidesplitter.

FIERY COMET

Cynthia Cooper and the Houston Comets cleaned up again at the WNBA finals. Cooper repeated as season MVP and playoff MVP and was fitted for her second championship ring. The league cleaned up too: Season ticket sales were up 72 percent; merchandise revenue tripled; expansion teams in Minnesota and Florida are in the works. But the real measure of success is the arrival of a WNBA Barbie.

JACKSON ACTION

Small spenders may not have noted the transformation of $50 and $100 bills, but this year the new $20 arrived. It has security features (polymer thread, microprinting, watermarking, color-shifting ink) that make it tough to counterfeit. On the other hand, its ugly.

THE COMEBACK TRAIL

An unprecedented number of previously threatened plants and animals are now flourishing and may soon be taken off the Department of the Interior's endangered species list. They include the peregrine falcon and the bald eagle (left).

TAKEN TO THE CLEANERS

The Starr report earned an X rating with a salacious selection of testimony from Monica Lewinsky. Photographs and other artifacts related to the impeachment recommendation, including the much-discussed blue dress, were also released to the media.

HIGHS AND LOWS

After nine months of storms, floods and heat waves, we've figured out who our friends are: More than 55 percent of Americans now regularly turn to the Weather Channel.

WHO *ARE* THESE PEOPLE?

Missed the *Jerry Springer Show* again? Here's the lineup from one summer week:

War of the Past Guests

Love Springer Style

Stop Sleeping With My Man!

Mom, Will You Marry Me?

Secret Bisexual Affairs

THE POTOMAC WATCH

"When I have made a friendship with someone, I remain that person's friend no matter which office he or she holds or doesn't hold."

Czech President Vaclav Havel, on whether Clinton's troubles will influence their personal relationship

"The President betrayed his wife. He did not betray the country. God help this nation if we fail to recognize the difference."

Rep. Robert Wexler, a Florida Democrat, on why he is opposed to impeachment proceedings

"I made a bad mistake. It was indefensible, and I'm sorry about it."

President Clinton, while on a trip to Ireland, making his first real apology for the Lewinsky affair

"I'm having one now."

Mrs. Clinton, on vacation in Martha's Vineyard, Mass., shortly after the President's "inappropriate contact" admission, when asked if she had ever taken a stress test

"I'm really sorry for everything that's happened. And I hate Linda Tripp."

Monica Lewinsky, in grand jury testimony

HELL NO, WE WON'T GO
Chicago police clubbed and gassed
demonstrators at the Democratic
Convention. Students protested Columbia
University's ties to the war effort.

1968

Thirty years ago, a surge of defiance
shook the Western world. In 1968,
the emblematic decade's emblem year,
citizens took to the streets with such
powerful purpose that their actions
threatened or changed regimes in France,
Czechoslovakia, Egypt and Belgium.
In the United States, riots destroyed
many inner cities, the war in Vietnam
provoked both raging demonstrations
and pacifist vigils, and assassins struck
down two men who bore the promise of
resolution: presidential candidate Robert
F. Kennedy and civil rights leader Dr.
Martin Luther King Jr.

TO THE BARRICADES

In France, student protests escalated; workers seized factories nationwide. In Paris, one May day, riot police battled 30,000 demonstrators.

PEACE PARADE

After the January Tet offensive, student radicals weren't the only ones demonstrating against the Vietnam war. The very people fighting the war, and veterans of earlier wars, marched in this San Francisco protest.

OLYMPIC POWER

At the 1968 Summer Olympics in Mexico City, Tommie Smith and John Carlos ran first and third in a record-setting 200-meter race. Both were suspended from the U.S. team after raising their fists in a black power salute during the medal ceremony.

PRAGUE SPRING

Alexander Dubcek's reforms seemed to hold infinite promise for Czechoslovakia—until the Russian tanks rolled in. In August, Warsaw Pact troops, 650,000 strong, restored the Soviet notion of "order" to what had been a burgeoning spring.

JOHN GLENN'S FINAL FRONTIER

The 77-year-old passed the same rigorous physical exam as the younger astronauts.

Glenn will tell you that Annie, his wife of 55 years, "has more guts" than anyone. He should know: They grew up together. Center: President Kennedy visited Glenn at Cape Canaveral, then invited him to Washington for honors that included a parade. Opposite: Straitlaced, yes, but Glenn and the other Mercury astronauts have clearly loved their work.

"Listen, Colonel, we are really proud of you and . . . you did a wonderful job."—President John F. Kennedy, 1962

To put it mildly, his family was unenthusiastic about his return to space. His beloved wife, Annie, had suffered through the gut-wrenching launch and reentry of the 1962 flight and did not look forward to repeating the experience. His son, David, a physician, was even more adamant. Perhaps because he had a professional understanding of the physical strains his 77-year-old dad would endure in orbit, he was flat against the idea.

But John Glenn turned on the freckle-faced smile and the smalltown Ohio charm and eventually won them over, just as he had NASA when he first proposed joining the space shuttle crew as a way to study the similarities between the effects of aging and the effects of space flight.

The whole family watched the late October launch—David, Annie, daughter Lynn and two grandkids (for whom Glenn had hung in his Senate office an old-geezer cartoon of the shuttle hurtling through space with a bumper sticker that read LET ME TELL YOU ABOUT MY GRANDCHILDREN). Also at the Kennedy Space Center were an astonishing 250,000 cheering spectators, the biggest crowd in years.

Before the flight, Glenn trained without complaint for months, admitting that he wasn't nearly as worried about blowing up as about screwing up his 12 onboard scientific experiments. By all accounts, he did fine. His job included collecting urine and blood samples from

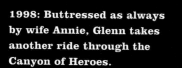

1998: Buttressed as always
by wife Annie, Glenn takes
another ride through the
Canyon of Heroes.

"Let the record show, John has a smile on his face and it goes from ear to ear."
—Lt. Col. Curtis L. Brown Jr., in orbit, 1998

the six other crew members and donating his own as well. (Glenn hates needles and took to calling the colleague who drew the blood "Count Dracula.")

Glenn also pasted sensors all over his head and torso before turning in, so his sleep patterns could be monitored, and took pictures with a digital camera and downloaded them to a NASA Web site. He answered questions from a group of students back on Earth, and even traded jokes on camera with Jay Leno. "This is the most amazing thing that has ever happened to me," Leno told the *Discovery* crew. "I had to write a paper on Senator Glenn in the sixth grade, and I can finally turn it in."

When the shuttle landed after 134 orbits, 3.6 million miles and nine days of weightlessness, Glenn was a tad unsteady. But he recovered quickly and a week and a half later was treated to the second New York City ticker-tape parade of his life. What the flight reveals about aging will take study. What it reveals about the man is already clear. "Hail, Columbia! happy land!" the poet Joseph Hopkinson wrote in 1798, precisely 200 years before Glenn's latest thrust into space. "Hail, ye heroes! heaven-born band!"

FALL

Miles to Go

Police say after two men targeted Matthew Shepard as gay, they robbed and pistol-whipped him, fracturing his skull. Then, on a near-freezing night, they lashed the University of Wyoming student to a fence and left him there. Russell Henderson (left) and Aaron McKinney are charged with the murder. Shepard's terrible death prompted calls for tolerance, but outside his funeral a protester's sign read GOD HATES FAGS.

108

ED ANDRIESKI/AP

OCT. 7 Epidemiologists report that the number of **AIDS deaths in the U.S. fell** nearly 50 percent last year, owing largely to powerful combination drug therapies. But public health officials advise continued caution because the rate of new HIV infections has not declined over the past several years.

OCT. 8 The House of Representatives votes 258–176 to begin an **impeachment investigation** of President Clinton that could extend beyond charges in the Starr report. While most House Democrats oppose an open-ended inquiry, only five vote against a probe of any kind.

OCT. 13 The National Basketball Association **cancels the first 99 games** of the new season because of a labor dispute between the players' union and team owners over salary caps and the distribution of league revenues. When talks stall in November, several owners acknowledge that the season may be lost.

Tableau of Terror

Enveloped by the stench of death at a newly discovered mass grave in northern Bosnia, forensic pathologists exhumed the decomposed bodies of 274 Muslims, believed to be early victims of brutal "ethnic cleansing" by Serbs. The corpses— some with mouths open in a last scream— were then laid out in front of a local mortuary to await identification by relatives. There, recovered vestiges of their lives glinted in the autumn sun: a pair of spectacles, prayer beads, a silver watch.

AMEL EMRIC
ASSOCIATED PRESS

OCT. 14 The FBI charges fugitive Eric Robert Rudolph, 32, with planting bombs at Centennial Olympic Park in 1996 and two other Atlanta-area sites in 1997. Rudolph joined **the FBI's Ten Most Wanted list** earlier this year as the sole suspect in the January bombing of a Birmingham, Ala., abortion clinic.

OCT. 17 When a spark ignites petroleum from a ruptured pipeline in Nigeria, **a massive fireball** engulfs hundreds of villagers. Among the estimated 1,000 dead are men, women and children who were siphoning gasoline at the site of the explosion.

OCT. 17 A deadly storm delivers heavy rain and tornadoes to Texas. Swollen rivers and creeks cause flash flooding across the southeastern part of the state. When **the slow-moving storm** finally weakens four days later, 29 people are dead and 20 counties are declared a federal disaster area.

Two Murders, No Peace

Mourners' sobs filled the air at a West Bank funeral as Chilean-born Jewish immigrant Danny Vargas, 28, was laid to rest. After his battered body was hurled from a speeding car in the bitterly divided city of Hebron, Palestinian medics labored furiously to resuscitate the Israeli soccer coach and father of two. Just hours later, in what may have been a retaliatory killing, a 68-year-old Palestinian farmer was found slain in his olive grove.

113

OCT. 19 The government's antitrust trial against Microsoft opens with lawyers assailing **the credibility of Microsoft CEO Bill Gates.** Presenting E-mails from Gates and other company executives, attorney David Boies argues that Microsoft orchestrated a deliberate strategy to "crush" Internet competitor Netscape.

OCT. 19 Mike Tyson's boxing license is restored by the Nevada State Athletic Commission after a team of psychiatrists and psychologists declares him mentally fit to fight. **Tyson had been barred** from the ring for biting Evander Holyfield's ears during their heavyweight championship bout in June 1997.

OCT. 21 President Clinton signs into law a **$500 billion federal budget** so unwieldy that many lawmakers complain they had no time to review the 40-pound, 3,825-page document before voting on it. The bill includes funding to hire 100,000 teachers and $17.9 billion for the International Monetary Fund, in addition to such pork-laden provisions as special breaks for oil companies and funds to research low-bush blueberries.

Rock of Ages

Imagine holding your breath for 1,600 years. That's how long Cleopatra's father, Ptolemy XII, or rather this granite sphinx with his face, spent at the bottom of Alexandria Bay. French marine archaeologists made the sensational discovery while exploring submerged ruins of the royal quarters where Cleopatra dreamed and schemed. Egyptian officials now envision the world's first underwater antiquities museum at this site, a place where visitors would stroll through glass-walled tunnels to view treasures still scattered on the seafloor.

114

OCT. 23 A sniper's bullet kills Dr. Barnett Slepian, an obstetrician-gynecologist who performed abortions in a Buffalo clinic, at his home in Amherst, N.Y. Canadian investigators believe Dr. Slepian's murder is linked to four other antiabortion shootings since 1994 in western New York and Canada. "It's really **an act of terrorism** and, in my mind, a cold-blooded assassination," says New York Governor George Pataki.

OCT. 26 New York Mets catcher Mike Piazza, 30, becomes the **highest-paid baseball player in history** when he signs a contract that will average $13 million annually over the next seven years.

OCT. 27 NATO backs away from its threat of air strikes against Yugoslavia after that nation substantially complies with U.N. demands and **withdraws forces** from many strongholds in Kosovo. Meanwhile, rebel soldiers begin to move into the vacated Serb positions.

Pinstripers on Parade

In lower Manhattan's Canyon of Heroes, two million Yankee fans turned out to see the World Series champs showered with glory—and 50 tons of confetti, shredded phone books and toilet paper. Financial district office workers enjoyed a nice vantage point from which to view crowd favorites in the sun-drenched blizzard: parade leader Darryl Strawberry in a red convertible, just nine days after colon cancer surgery; cutie-pie shortstop Derek Jeter; and pitcher Orlando Hernández, fresh from a predawn visit with his mother and two daughters flown in from Cuba. That joyful reunion came 10 months— and a record 125 Bronx Bomber victories— after El Duque fled his homeland.

OCT. 31 Iraq announces it will deny U.N. weapons inspectors access to monitoring sites. Despite harsh condemnations from the U.N. Security Council, **Iraq says it won't back down,** even under threat of force, until economic sanctions are lifted.

NOV. 1 Defending champion John Kagwe, 29, of Kenya wins the **New York City Marathon** in 2 hours 8 minutes 45 seconds—the fifth-fastest time in the event's history. Franca Fiacconi, 33, kisses the finish line after she becomes the first Italian woman to win the race.

NOV. 3 Despite Republican hopes for gains in this midterm election, **Democrats pick up five House seats** and suffer no losses in the Senate. GOP leaders blame a campaign strategy that focused on the Clinton–Lewinsky affair instead of issues like taxes, Social Security and education.

After the Apocalypse

In Honduras, floodwaters swept away entire Tegucigalpa neighborhoods and destroyed 70 percent of the country's key crops. In Nicaragua, the rain-swollen crater of Casitas Volcano collapsed, burying four villages in an avalanche of mud. Such was the devastation wreaked by Hurricane Mitch, the area's deadliest storm in 200 years. This youngster being handed to a relief worker in Ciudad Dario, north of Managua, was among the lucky—many of the more than 12,000 victims were children. Those who escaped drowning or entombment in mud wandered starving, to die from diseases spread by rotting corpses and foul water.

119

RODRIGO ARANGUA
AFP

NOV. 5 Ending nearly 200 years of squabbling among scholars, the journal *Nature* reports that DNA tests on blood samples taken from **descendants of Thomas Jefferson and one of his slaves,** Sally Hemings, almost certainly prove that America's third President fathered Hemings's youngest son, Eston.

NOV. 6 Scientists announce the first cultivation of human embryonic stem cells, a medical breakthrough that could lead to **tissue regeneration** and new gene therapies. These manufactured cells—with the potential to form many human tissues—invite debate on the ethical implications of emerging biotechnology.

NOV. 6 In the wake of the Republicans' unexpected midterm election losses, **Newt Gingrich resigns** as speaker of the House and announces he will retire from Congress. Hours earlier, Rep. Bob Livingston of Louisiana had announced a challenge to Gingrich's leadership.

Monk vs. Monk

"Are you monks or hoodlums?" shouted shocked observers at Seoul's Chogye Temple, headquarters for South Korea's largest Buddhist denomination. Trading meditation for mayhem, rival factions of monks—and black-clothed bodyguards—kicked and punched one another. Followers of one spiritual leader ripped out steel-framed windows of the pagoda-shaped building occupied by a rival and his fire-extinguisher-wielding loyalists. At issue: an election to determine the next general secretariat, who is in charge of naming leaders at 1,700 Zen sanctuaries of peace and enlightenment.

121

NOV. 10 A California appeals court overturns a 1996 **ruling that gave O.J. Simpson full custody** of his youngest children, Sydney, 13, and Justin, 10, saying the lower court judge should have allowed evidence that Simpson may have murdered his former wife. The kids are reportedly "very disappointed" with the decision.

NOV. 13 Monica Lewinsky signs a **$600,000-plus book deal** with St. Martin's Press to tell her story. Lewinsky also agrees to an interview, for which she will not be paid, with Barbara Walters of ABC News.

NOV. 13 Admitting no wrongdoing, President Clinton agrees to pay Paula Jones $850,000 to **drop her sexual harassment lawsuit** against him. The settlement amounts to only a portion of Jones's legal bills.

A WARNING TO TYRANTS

Recuperating after back surgery, Gen. Augusto Pinochet was arrested in bed at a London hospital. A Spanish judge charged Chile's former dictator with "crimes of genocide and terrorism that include murder." A demonstrator waved the Chilean flag in Trafalgar Square while the House of Lords weighed a High Court ruling that the arrest was unlawful because of sovereign immunity. On Pinochet's 83rd birthday in late November, a 3–2 majority handed down the verdict: no immunity. He will remain under police guard while Spain seeks extradition.

122

NOV. 14 At 8:45 a.m., minutes away from secretly firing hundreds of cruise missiles against Iraq, President Clinton delays the attack when Iraq suddenly announces that U.N. weapons inspectors will be allowed to resume work. **A tense debate ensues** at the White House, but after pledges of unconditional cooperation from Iraq, the President finally calls off the air strikes around three a.m. the next day.

NOV. 17 In a somber vote, Israel's parliament approves a **land-for-security peace accord** with the Palestinians. The deal gives Palestinians a portion of the West Bank's occupied territory in return for assurances that the Palestinian Authority will crack down on terrorism against Israel.

NOV. 20 Russia launches Zarya, the first component of a $35 billion space station that the U.S. and 15 other countries plan to construct **220 miles above Earth.** Building the enormous habitable complex will require dozens of space flights, 960 hours of spacewalking and nearly 900,000 pounds of supplies.

Zero-G and Feeling Fine

President and Hillary Clinton sharing binoculars at Cape Canaveral, body boarders, visitors jamming beaches and just about anyone with access to a TV— all were transfixed at 2:19 p.m. on a bright October day by *Discovery*'s spectacular liftoff. Rocket boosters fired and withholding clamps exploded as the shuttle blasted into space at 9,000 mph, trailing white vapor on a cerulean slate and awakening a nation's dormant love of space travel. Along with a certain payload specialist who joked that he favored Metamucil-laced Tang, the crew included a rookie astronaut from Spain and the cardiovascular surgeon who had been Japan's first woman in space.

125

NOV. 24 The U.S. Consumer Product Safety Commission recalls 9.6 million playpens because they pose **a risk of strangulation**. Loose clothing and pacifier strings that snagged on protruding rivets have caused eight toddler deaths since 1983, according to the commission.

DEC. 1 Oil behemoths Exxon and Mobil propose a $75 billion merger that would create **the world's biggest company**, one that would surpass General Motors in annual sales.

DEC. 8 Electrical workers accidentally cause a **massive blackout** in San Francisco, stranding subway passengers, disrupting air travel, shutting down some businesses and leaving nearly a million people without power for six hours.

DEC. 11 The journal *Science* reports that biologists have mapped **the entire genetic code** of the nematode worm, the first genome of a multicellular organism to be fully sequenced. Because mammals share many of the worm's 20,000 genes, it is hoped the decoding will advance understanding of the human blueprint.

It's a Wrap

In a Swiss park, winter light shimmered through translucent shrouds that transformed 178 trees—oak, plum, cherry, gingko, beech and golden weeping willow— into works of art. The realization of a 30-year dream of artists Christo and Jeanne-Claude, his wife, the project required 592,000 square feet of gauzy fabric secured by 14 miles of rope. Folks, you earned it: Take a bough.

126

DEC. 12 Trumping Mo Vaughn and Mike Piazza, baseball's former top-earning players, pitcher Kevin Brown signs a **$105 million, seven-year contract** with the Los Angeles Dodgers.

DEC. 16 President Clinton launches air strikes against Iraq less than 24 hours after learning that Saddam Hussein's government had failed once again to cooperate with U.N. weapons inspectors. The U.S. House almost unanimously supports **the military action**, but some Republicans question the timing of the attack, which comes on the eve of the scheduled impeachment vote.

DEC. 20 Nkem Chukwu, 27, gives birth to the only known **living set of octuplets** in the world. Five girls and two boys are born almost two weeks after the first baby girl was delivered. The infants' total weight is a shade over 10 pounds, and they are listed in critical condition.

Marching into History

A seemingly endless process, initiated years ago with Kenneth Starr's Whitewater investigation, climaxed in one dizzying and dramatic day. Voting along almost straight party lines, the House of Representatives impeached President Clinton for perjury and obstruction of justice in the Monica Lewinsky affair. Hours before, House Speaker–designate and recently confessed adulterer Robert Livingston had called for the President's resignation and, greeted by Democrats' jeers of "*You* resign," stunned Congress by doing just that. Bolstered by the First Lady's eleventh-hour support and high approval ratings, Clinton made his way through the White House portico to address the press. He vowed to remain "until the last hour of the last day of my term."

129

ATTENTION, SHOPPERS
In demand? That doesn't *begin* to describe the frenzy over Furby! F.A.O. Schwarz was fielding 12,000 phone calls a day for the ticklish toy; more than a million Furbys flew out of stores; Web sites scalped them at quadruple the list price. For the thoroughly fed up, there was even a Furby Autopsy Web site. Merry Christmas.

THE FALL REPORT

OCTOBER NOVEMBER DECEMBER

Owing in some measure to the workings of El Niño, 1998 turned out to be America's worst year on record for natural disasters: ice storms, tornadoes, floods, fires, droughts and hurricanes. Another sort of disaster, Saddam Hussein, unleashed mayhem again this year, causing anguish for his people and frustration for the international community. Clinton could order bombs to quiet Hussein, but he could not quell the firestorm in Washington. Yet despite natural and man-made calamities, the American spirit finds reason to give thanks. For example, that the McCaughey septuplets had a healthy and happy first birthday. That in Ireland and Israel there have been intimations of peace. And that a new year always brings new hope.

> ## "It's too bad he lives in the city. He's depriving some small village of a pretty good idiot."
>
> Mike Milbury, New York Islanders general manager, on agent Paul Kraus, whose client Zigmund Palffy had rejected several salary offers from the Isles

WHAT A CROC!

A dig in Niger's Tenere desert has revealed a previously unknown species of dinosaur that lived 100 million years ago. *Suchomimus tenerensis* grew to about 36 feet in length and had 16-inch curved thumb claws and a crocodilelike snout. It ran on its hind legs and—according to a *Chicago Tribune* writer who may have been thinking of Mark McGwire—had "powerful Popeye-like forearms."

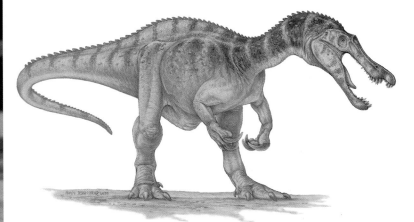

AMAZING GRACE

At Grenoble's Winter Olympics in 1968, a runner-up said of the gold medal figure skater that "everything Peggy does is pure ballerina." Thirty years later, it's still true. Now a TV commentator, 50-year-old Peggy Fleming underwent treatment for breast cancer this year. Then, in an effort to marshal forces against the disease, the five-time U.S. champion shared her story with the world.

SUGARY SCEPTERS

Outside St. Peter's Basilica in Rome, souvenir stands marked John Paul II's 20th anniversary as pope by appealing to the sweet-toothed faithful.

> ## "What Saddam is hearing now are the sounds of silence. No one is standing up to defend him, to argue on his behalf or to help him out of the hole he's dug himself."
>
> State Department spokesman James P. Rubin, on the international response to Iraq's refusal to allow weapons inspections

FUN-RAISING AFLOAT

Clear the decks! To raise money for the local Red Cross chapter, some 40,000 incognito rubber ducks (each was numbered on the bottom) rode the currents of the Singapore River at what can be described only as a stately pace: The winning duckie clocked in at 1.9 mph.

OUR GOVERNOR CAN BEAT UP YOUR GOVERNOR

Bumper sticker seen in Minnesota after Jesse "the Body" Ventura (below), former pro wrestler, was elected governor in November

A GLIMPSE OF THE FUTURE

The Post Office has some sticker shock in store for us. In early '99, Priority Mail's space shuttle stamp will carry a $3.20 price tag. Regular postage will rise by one cent, the value of this transitional "makeup" stamp.

The "H" Rate make-up stamp — USA

$3.20 USA

TRUE COLORS

We thought we knew what Saturn looked like. But the Hubble Space Telescope continued its eye-opening ways this year, revealing at last the lovely, romantic pastels that are produced when ultraviolet light from the sun shines on Saturn's unromantic methane gas.

> "People have said, 'What are you going to do when they're all sixteen and they all want a car?' They'll get a job!"

Bobbi McCaughey, mother of septuplets who celebrated their first birthday on November 19

RUBBER DUCKS: ROSLAN RAHMAN/AFP; JESSE VENTURA: TIM DILLON/USA TODAY; SATURN: HUBBLE HERITAGE TEAM/NASA

PRESIDENTURE MATTERS

The bicentennial of George Washington's death is in 1999, but special events got under way early and included cleaning and restoring his D.C. monument (right). A traveling exhibit, "Treasures from Mount Vernon," featured Washington's legendary false teeth (below). They include human and bovine teeth and ones carved from elephant tusk. All are set in a lead-alloy base and connected by heavy steel springs, a combination the wearer found "uneasy in the mouth."

WARM WHEELS

A little too warm, actually. Some of Fisher-Price's 10 million Power Wheels for two- to seven-year-olds had a problem with overheating and needed a recall. The company made repairs and—should we be grateful?—got our kids back on the road.

"Half the members here couldn't lift it, let alone read it."

Oregon Democrat Peter DeFazio, on the 40-pound, $500 billion federal budget

WYLE E. COYOTE

THE POTOMAC WATCH

"We're like Wyle E. Coyote. We've strapped on the rockets, and now we're headed straight for a wall."

A Republican staffer, on his party's push to continue impeachment proceedings against the President

"The answer to the big question is no, I have not been unfaithful to my spouse."

Independent Counsel Kenneth Starr, to Diane Sawyer on *20/20*

"If I ever want to have an affair with a married man again, especially if he's President, please shoot me."

Monica Lewinsky, on the phone to Linda Tripp, during a taped conversation

"He is an enormously gifted and richly qualified leader . . . but someone who is exasperatingly stupid in his personal life."

Former White House spokesman Mike McCurry

Dancers at the American Lindy Hop
Championships included professionals like
(counterclockwise from top) Roddy Caravella
and Midori Asakura, Angie Whitworth and
Bill Kline, and Janice Wilson and Paolo
Lanna; and amateurs like graphic designer
Dan Cavaliere, who couldn't imagine a
better Halloween weekend.

SWINGIN'

It got cooking nearly a decade ago at
the Deluxe, San Francisco's art deco
nightclub. Hipsters in their vintage
best improvised a lively "street" swing
to the beat of early masters like Cab
Calloway and Louis Jordan. The
acrobatic lindy hop, born in Harlem's
Savoy Ballroom in the 1920s, came
bopping back, thanks in part to a TV
ad featuring fresh-faced kids jivin'
to Louis Prima. At the first (yes, the
first, amazingly enough) American
Lindy Hop Championships, held this
October in McAfee, N.J., contestants'
euphoric smiles told the whole secret
of swing: pure joy.

PHOTOGRAPHY BY DIETMAR BUSSE

When it comes to the lindy, age doesn't matter. Couples in their seventies shared the floor with teenagers. Carnell Pipkin, 46, and Tena Morales, 39 (bottom left), got a standing ovation for their groovin' performance. Best friends Nina Gilkenson, 14, and Naomi Uyama, 17 (bottom right, with friend Steve Cowles, 21), took up swing to impress a boy in a local rockabilly band; now they're winning competitions. As for the boy, "We're over him now," says Naomi.

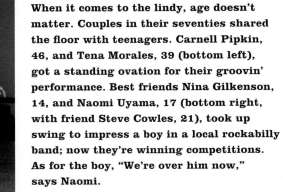

TRIBUTES

Frank Sinatra 1915–1998 The high school
dropout from Hoboken, N.J., knew in his twenties what top-of-
the-heap felt like. "Nobody's ever been a bigger star than me,"
he said. "This'll never end." It almost did, though, lots of times.
The scandalous behavior—the punch-outs with paparazzi, the
affair with Ava Gardner—put his career in the dumps. It almost
ended when Sinatra, desolate over losing Ava, put his head in
the oven. The guy was often at the brink but always came back.
Now it seems he was right all along—it'll never end. "There's
no void," said his dear friend Tony Bennett as he sat in an Italian
restaurant reminiscing about Sinatra. "You see, it's not that
way with musicians. They leave behind the music, which will live
forever. We'll never lose Sinatra." Bennett paused, took a sip
of wine and continued: "I'm reminded of the day Gershwin died.
One of his friends was told about it, and he just stared: 'Gershwin
died,' he said. And then he said, 'I don't have to believe that.'"

PETER MARTIN

Sonny Bono 1935–1998 He will always be remembered as the shorter half of Sonny and Cher—as a nasal-voiced, goofy-banged Everyman whose partnership with a pop goddess seemed a cosmic gag. But Bono wrote the stuff that made the couple stars, from their 1965 hit "I Got You Babe" to the put-downs his spouse rained on him on *The Sonny and Cher Comedy Hour.* After their breakup in 1974, he recast himself as a restaurateur, then—improbably—as a Republican politician. The self-deprecating congressman from Palm Springs died in a skiing accident. He was succeeded in office by his fourth wife, Mary, and eulogized by his second: "He had the confidence to be the butt of the joke," said Cher, "because he created the joke."

Tammy Wynette 1942–1998 Her life was loaded with pain—which helped make Tammy Wynette one of the greatest country divas of all time. Her best-loved songs are about enduring hardship and living on: the defeated lover in "Apartment #9"; the understanding wife in "Stand By Your Man"; and the loving mother mourning a marriage's end in "D-I-V-O-R-C-E." Wynette was married five times, most famously to country-music legend George Jones. In 1978 she seemed to find happiness with George Richey, but her medical woes (resulting in at least 17 major surgeries) continued, as did bouts with depression. Still, she went on, writing, singing, performing. In April, Tammy Wynette died in her sleep. "She had a tough life," a friend said. "She deserved an easy death."

NORMAN SEEFF
ASYLUM

Robert Young 1907–1998 He played classic, all-American, dependable fellows, his smile so charming you'd trust him with your life. Many remember him for his TV roles: dad Jim Anderson on *Father Knows Best* and the lovable healer Marcus Welby, M.D. But Young lit up the big screen, too, acting in more than 100 films, often—he once quipped— as the square who could never remove his dinner jacket. Beloved even for his Sanka ads, Young successfully hid his demons—the battles with alcohol and depression—from the camera, and remained a good doctor to millions.

Henny Youngman 1906–1998 His trademark violin and rapid-fire punchlines continued to zing to the end. After spending 70-odd years in show business, the irreplaceable Henny Youngman had the chutzpah to call his autobiography *Take My Life, Please!* Nobody had his skill with a joke and his spectacular speed of wit. Youngman's death, in February, calls for a paraphrasing of one of his own lines: "His absence makes us long for his presence."

Benjamin Spock 1903–1998 For decades, experts urged parents to ignore their instincts, preaching that infants must be fed on a strict schedule, must never be hugged or kissed. Then, in 1946, came *Baby and Child Care*. "Trust yourself," the book began. "You know more than you think you do." Emphasizing flexibility and affection, Dr. Spock's manual covered everything from croup to sibling rivalry and sparked a revolution in child-rearing. Critics blamed the protests of the '60s on children spoiled by Spock. (The former Republican joined those protests himself and ran for President on a left-wing ticket.) Yet moms and dads around the world still swear by his bible: By the time of his death, it had sold 50 million copies in 42 languages.

Betty Carter 1929–1998 She employed only young talent to back her and fostered the careers of legends-to-be like drummer Max Roach and pianist Mulgrew Miller, who honored her with music at her funeral. It was a fitting tribute to "Betty Bebop," who did it her way, mesmerizing audiences with bold improvisations and heart-melting balladry, and paying the price (her first major record deal and Grammy came 43 years after she began singing in Detroit clubs). "What is jazz?" someone once asked her. "If you come to see me," she replied, "you'll find out."

Linda McCartney 1941–1998 Linda Eastman broke more hearts than Helen of Troy when she wed the world's cutest Beatle. But Paul McCartney's jealous fans consoled themselves with the thought that it wouldn't last; celebrity marriages never do. This one did—for 29 years. "The bottom line is that we love each other, and what's more, we like each other," her husband said. But she was much more than Paul's wife: An acclaimed photographer and a tireless activist on behalf of animals, she wrote two cookbooks and even started her own line of vegetarian dinners. As she lay ill with breast cancer, Paul urged her to imagine herself on her beautiful Appaloosa stallion, surrounded by bluebells. With this paradisiacal image in her mind, Linda McCartney died.

Alan Shepard 1923–1998 Someone had to go first. Even among the seven Mercury astronauts, instant American heroes, one man had to become the first to ride the tower of flame to the edge of Earth's atmosphere and beyond. Alan Shepard launched a golf shot on the surface of the moon and, later, a successful career as a businessman. He and his wife, Louise, died within weeks of each other this summer, their sights set firmly on the stars.

DAN BORRIS
OUTLINE PRESS

Gene Autry 1907–1998 Everyone knows the greatest entertainers are awarded a star on the Hollywood Walk of Fame. By that measure, Gene Autry of tiny Tioga, Tex., was the greatest entertainer in history: He has *five*. One was for his recordings (among them, "Rudolph the Red-Nosed Reindeer"); one for his long-running radio show; one for his TV show; one for his countless live performances; and one for his 90-plus movies. He was equally successful as a business tycoon: "Autry used to ride off into the sunset," a friend said in later years. "Now he owns it." Yet his greatest achievement was Gene Autry's Cowboy Code, a set of values he passed on to millions of American youngsters. "The cowboy must . . . Never go back on his word . . . Be gentle with children, the elderly and animals. Not advocate or possess racially or religiously intolerant ideas. Help people in distress. Be a good worker . . . Be a patriot." Hollywood hokum? Gene Autry lived it.

DAVID SUTTON
MPTV

Barry Goldwater 1909–1998 Running for
President in 1964, he expected to lose big to Lyndon Baines
Johnson. So Barry Morris Goldwater, Arizona senator and retired
businessman, turned his campaign into a crusade for individual
freedom. Many of his "right wing" ideas seemed downright
kooky, even dangerous, at the time. When conservatism went
mainstream some 16 years later, served up by Ronald Reagan,
Goldwater was less than delighted. The Republican iconoclast
bristled at his party's moral fervor and publicly declared his
support for abortion and gay rights. He said, with typical candor,
"If they don't like it, to hell with them."

371

Harry Caray 1919–1998 He was as beloved a fixture at Wrigley Field as the ivy on the outfield wall. Announcer Harry Christopher Caray (born Carabina) hung out of the press box and bellowed "Take Me Out to the Ball Game" during the seventh-inning stretch at every Chicago Cubs home game (he had worked for the White Sox earlier). His voice was awful, his love for the game immense and pure. He was honored by the Baseball Hall of Fame in 1989 without ever putting on a glove. As Harry would say, "Holy cow!"

Florence Griffith Joyner 1959–1998
At the opening of the 1988 U.S. Olympic trials, Florence Griffith Joyner was a competitor. At the Games' close, she was a phenomenon. Over the course of that summer, she annihilated the women's 100-meter world record, won three gold medals, sprinted the fastest 200 meters in history and anchored the 1,600-meter silver-medal relay team. She was hailed as the greatest female athlete ever. With her unparalleled strength and speed—and her racy bodysuits and elaborate nails—Flo-Jo blended athleticism, feminism and glamour. In two months, she did more to revolutionize women's sports than everyone before her and anyone since. This fall she had a seizure and suffocated in her sleep. Her records and her legacy still stand.

149

George Wallace 1919–1998

He was short and pugnacious; even his pompadour had a cocky tilt to it. His mouth wore a permanent sneer, as if wrapped around a cigar even when it wasn't. Yet George Wallace had a certain dangerous charm. He was a vicious race-baiter when it could win him the Alabama governorship, but when he campaigned for the presidency, he came off more as a piney-woods populist, whacking away good-naturedly at the "pointy-headed intellectuals" in Washington. After a would-be assassin's bullet partially paralyzed him, he began to gentle, even admitting that segregation had been a mistake. His turnaround on race may have been pragmatic, but it was graceful. Amazing.

Eldridge Cleaver 1935–1998 He was a self-confessed rapist who became America's emblem of black empowerment in the 1960s, a self-educated man who wrote a best-selling prison memoir called *Soul on Ice*. In truth, Eldridge Cleaver's was on fire for most of his 62 years. He was the minister of information for the Black Panther party, striking a pose—in black beret and black leather jacket—that shook up white America. After a gunfight with Oakland police, he jumped bail and fled to Algeria. In 1975 he saw a blinding light that led him to Christianity and back to the United States. He became a Republican, endorsed Ronald Reagan, opened a boutique that sold trousers with codpieces and battled an addiction to crack cocaine. When he died of cancer in May, his wanderings came to an end, his soul on ice at last.

GORDON PARKS

Lloyd Bridges 1913–1998 "If you're doing something you really love, you can do it forever," Lloyd Bridges once said, and he did—in his career and his personal life. An actor of rare staying power, he'll be remembered for work in films ranging from *High Noon* to *Airplane!* But to TV-tuned baby boomers he'll always be Mike Nelson, the scuba-diving detective who took families on weekly underwater adventures in *Sea Hunt*, the show that gave his boys, Beau and Jeff, their acting starts. A devoted paterfamilias who made acting a family affair, Bridges had just finished filming *Meeting Daddy* with Beau when he died at home with his wife of 59 years at his side.

152

Maureen O'Sullivan 1911–1998 Although she appeared in serious films like *Pride and Prejudice* and *Anna Karenina* and graced such Hollywood classics as *The Big Clock* and *A Day at the Races,* Maureen O'Sullivan will forever be thought of as Jane, the delightful consort of Tarzan of the Jungle. The Irish-born actress, a perfect foil to Johnny Weissmuller, brought a delicate beauty, casual sophistication and fetching innocence to six Tarzan flicks in the 1930s and '40s. In 1936 she married screenwriter and director John Farrow, with whom she had seven children. Their eldest daughter was named Maria but is better known today as Mia Farrow.

Roddy McDowall 1928–1998 No child actor
ever expressed grief more poignantly than young Roddy
McDowall, in movies like *Lassie Come Home* and the superb *How
Green Was My Valley*. One of the few child stars able to make the
harsh transition to mature performer, McDowall appeared in 130
films, often stealing scenes with his acutely eccentric manner. A
native of London, he and his family moved to Hollywood during
the 1940 Blitz. There, he became known as an uncommonly loyal
friend, most notably in a long, extraordinarily close relationship
with fellow British child star Elizabeth Taylor.

Roy Rogers 1911–1998 The "King of the Cowboys" reigned from the 1930s to the 1960s, a paragon in that long cinematic line of straight shooters who packed six-shooters only to subdue the forces of evil. And while not the first cowpoke to sing, Roy Rogers, né Leonard Slye, did have real musical talent, perhaps best displayed with his group the Sons of the Pioneers. His TV show costarred his longtime wife, Dale Evans (the "Queen of the West"), and beloved palomino, Trigger. By the 1950s the show had raised Roy Rogers to the status of icon—one with the decency and humility of yesteryear. Happy trails.

Fred Friendly 1915–1998 A broadcast journalist of Brobdingnagian proportions, Fred Friendly was too big for the box in which he spent much of his working life. Even the name— Ferdinand Friendly Wachenheimer—was too large and had to be shortened. As Edward R. Murrow's producer at CBS, he helped define the television news documentary. Their skewering of Sen. Joseph R. McCarthy, reporting on migrant farm workers in *Harvest of Shame* in 1960 and collaboration on *CBS Reports* earned them a prominent place in the pantheon of TV journalism. But his pride was outsize too: He quit as president of CBS News in 1966 when his superiors chose to air an *I Love Lucy* rerun instead of live coverage of a Senate hearing on Vietnam. Carl Sandburg once said of Friendly that he looked "as if he had just got off a foam-flecked horse." He continued tilting at the networks as a writer, journalism professor and host of television seminars until, weakened by strokes, he dismounted at 82.

James Earl Ray 1928–1998 A teacher once wrote on his report card, under Attitude Toward Regulations, "violates all of them." But no one could have foreseen the enormity of one of James Earl Ray's transgressions: In 1968 he killed a dream. Although he confessed to shooting Dr. Martin Luther King Jr. as the civil rights leader stood on the balcony of a Memphis motel in 1968, Ray soon recanted. He spent the next 30 years unsuccessfully trying to prove his innocence: A mysterious accomplice named "Raoul" never materialized, nor did any evidence of a conspiracy. When he died of liver failure, Ray still had 70 years of his sentence to serve.

157

Bella Abzug
1920–1998 Raspy-voiced and madly hatted, Bella Abzug ran for Congress by claiming "this woman's place is in the House." A stalwart proletarian with no airs about her, Abzug championed underdogs, battled vested interests and was an early voice in the call for Richard Nixon's impeachment.

E.G. Marshall
1910–1998 Can someone be born to play a lawyer? The veteran character actor seemed to become Lawrence Preston of *The Defenders*, a role for which he won two Emmys and the one we remember best. But Marshall actually had a wider legal range, notably in *Twelve Angry Men*, and as John Mitchell in 1995's *Nixon*.

Flip Wilson
1933–1998 "Here come da judge." "The devil made me do it." "What you see is what you get." The comedian moved on late in 1998, but the catchphrases will stay with us, made indelible by the man and his female alter ego, Geraldine. She "carried me longer than my mother did," Wilson once claimed, but he did all the heavy lifting.

Phil Hartman
1948–1998 For eight years, he was the glue (and the Frank Sinatra and the Bill Clinton) of the cast of *Saturday Night Live*. Recently, he had anchored the ensemble of actors on *NewsRadio* and taken small roles in more than 15 movies. Then the impossible: One night in late May, his third wife, Brynn, shot him; hours later she killed herself.

Tom Bradley
1917–1998 The son of Texas sharecroppers lived a life of memorable firsts: L.A.'s first black police lieutenant, first black city councilman, first black mayor (who wound up serving 20 years). In his devotion, he was also First Citizen of the city he loved.

Shari Lewis
1934–1998 A magician's daughter, the master puppeteer-ventriloquist had a few tricks up—and around— her own sleeve, most notably her sly, pun-loving costar Lamb Chop. Her books, recordings and TV series (for which she won five of her 12 Emmys) appealed to children of all ages.

Akira Kurosawa
1910–1998 To filmmakers, the great Japanese director was the emperor of the art house. His movies—from the Oscar-winning *Rashomon* to *The Seven Samurai* to the great battle pictures *Kagemusha* and *Ran*—are regarded as works of genius. Steven Spielberg called Kurosawa "the pictorial Shakespeare of our time."

Stokely Carmichael
1941–1998 Early in his activism, he embraced nonviolence, but the man who coined the phrase "black power" severed ties with the Black Panthers in 1969 because they weren't militant enough. With a new name, Kwame Ture, he moved to Guinea, where he continued to hope for an uprising to liberate African Americans.